If the prosperity gospel had a heart, Karen has stomped that sucker flat. Scouring the back roads between Portland, Oregon, and Pinehurst, North Carolina, Karen spins stories of unforgettable characters, including the two-fingered Ambassador and the nearly bankrupt Bookseller. Each encounter will test your heart and mind, pushing you into a conversation often avoided. Whether you live in a mansion on a cliff, a shack by still waters, or in a single-wide on cinder blocks, this is a worthy read.

WM. PAUL YOUNG, author of *The Shack*

★

I have been a "have" and a "have-not" in my life. I have found in my walk with the Lord, as Karen illustrates so well in these beautiful stories, that the riches he desires for us have nothing to do with money. I love a writer that's not afraid to walk with real people and speak the truth of their lives. Keep shining your light, Karen!

JEFF FOXWORTHY

★

[Karen Spears Zacharias has] a huge fan in the Allman Brothers Band of heathens. Thank you for being brave enough to stand up and be one of our prophets. We desperately need you.

OTEIL BURBRIDGE, bassist and vocalist, Allman Brothers Band

★

If Fanny Flagg got religion, she'd be Karen Spears Zacharias. Zacharias goes after the prosperity gospel not with a theological rebuttal but with stories about people who are living the real gospel: people who've loved big, lost big, and become 'the least of these' for the sake of Christ, and who are spiritually richer than any slick TV preacher will ever be. She is trailer-trash wonderful, a guilty pleasure: like eating chicken-fried steak with mac & cheese during Bible study.

SUSAN E. ISAACS, author of *Angry Conversations with God*

Tragedy, hilarity, and poignancy do a square dance together in Karen Spears Zacharias' latest offering. *Will Jesus Buy Me a Double-Wide?* gives us a Spirit-infused meditation on gratuitous wealth and barely gettin'by, all under the paradoxical canopy of the United States of America — a.k.a. Jesusland. Her portraits of the lonely rich, the happy poor, and everyone in between move beyond clichés to reveal a common humanity and a common grace to be found in faith, hope, and love. The stories will stay with you. Read this book and be changed.

MIKE MORRELL, zoecarnate.com and TheOOZE.com

★

Will Jesus Buy Me a Double-Wide? is a welcome remedy to the get-rich-quick theology of Jesus as banker. Zacharias shows us a different view of Christianity, and she does so with wisdom and compassion.

RON RASH, author of *Serena*

★

Karen Spears Zacharias turns her investigative journalist's eye on the shameless materialism of American Christianity and forcefully illustrates the error and the deception of the prosperity doctrine in all its forms and hues. She undercuts the gloss of the popular doctrine with funny, affecting stories of authentic American lives that range from millionaire bankers to humble trailer-dwellers and fingerless ham-radio evangelists, and she challenges the great lie inherent in the teaching that anyone, by any means, can manipulate the favor of the Almighty.

JANICE OWENS, author of *The Cracker Kitchen* and *The Schooling of Claybird Catts*

★

Behind this satirical title lies a book filled with insight and wisdom. Karen Spears Zacharias provides parables of people who confront their faith with truth and grit. It's an honest and timely read.

MICHAEL MORRIS, author of *Slow Way Home*

★

An honest, raw account of some who use God for their purposes and some who seek to allow God to use them — a huge difference!

REV. DR. LAYNE E. SMITH, senior pastor,
Viewmont Baptist Church, Hickory, North Carolina

★

Karen Spears Zacharias assembles a panorama of people who have been "blessed" by God, and then she dissects these blessings. This is religious research like you have never seen before, and it makes for fascinating reading.

JACKIE K. COOPER, author of *The Sunrise Remembers*

★

Karen Spears Zacharias' voice is one that needs to be heard as we all hit the reset button on the priorities in our lives. She says it best: "Peace, not prosperity, is what we ought to be pursuing." I couldn't agree more.

W. RALPH EUBANKS, author of *Ever Is a Long Time*
and *The House at the End of the Road*

★

Reading Karen Spears Zacharias is like sitting with an old friend on a porch swing, sipping sweet tea, unmindful of the skeeters because her stories are mesmerizing. They provoke laughter, tears, discomfort, and a deep quiet in the face of the Almighty, who is never, ever a formula.

SALLY JOHN, novelist of Safe Harbors Series and others

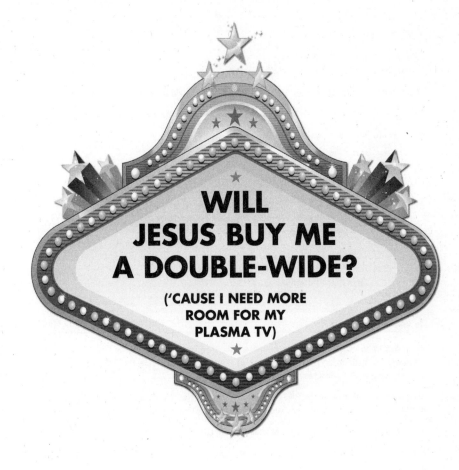

WILL JESUS BUY ME A DOUBLE-WIDE?

('CAUSE I NEED MORE ROOM FOR MY PLASMA TV)

KAREN SPEARS ZACHARIAS

ZONDERVAN®

ZONDERVAN.com/
AUTHORTRACKER
follow your favorite authors

ZONDERVAN

Will Jesus Buy Me a Double-Wide?
Copyright © 2010 by Karen Spears Zacharias

This title is also available as a Zondervan ebook. Visit www.zondervan.com/ebooks.

This title is also available in a Zondervan audio edition. Visit www.zondervan.fm.

Requests for information should be addressed to:
Zondervan, *Grand Rapids, Michigan 49530*

Library of Congress Cataloging-in-Publication Data

Zacharias, Karen Spears.
    Will Jesus buy me a double-wide? : ('cause I need more room for my plasma TV) /
Karen Spears Zacharias.
        p.   cm.
    Includes bibliographical references (p.).
    ISBN 978-0-310-29250-0 (hardcover, jacketed)
        1. Christian life—United States. 2. Money—Religious aspects—Christianity.
I. Title.
BR517.Z33 2010
261.8'50973—dc22   2009040185

All Scripture quotations, unless otherwise indicated, are taken from the Holy Bible, *New International Version®, NIV®.* Copyright © 1973, 1978, 1984 by Biblica, Inc.™ Used by permission of Zondervan. All rights reserved worldwide.

Scripture quotations marked NKJV are taken from the New King James Version. Copyright © 1982, by Thomas Nelson, Inc. Used by permission. All rights reserved.

Scripture quotations marked KJV are taken from the King James Version of the Bible.

Scripture on page 159 is the speaker's paraphrase.

Any Internet addresses (websites, blogs, etc.) and telephone numbers printed in this book are offered as a resource. They are not intended in any way to be or imply an endorsement by Zondervan, nor does Zondervan vouch for the content of these sites and numbers for the life of this book.

Cover design: *Laura Maitner-Mason*
Cover photos: *Ed Freeman, Getty Images / Jupiter Images*
Author photo: *Leslie Goldberg*
Interior design: *Beth Shagene*

Printed in the United States of America

09 10 11 12 13 14 • 24 23 22 21 20 19 18 17 16 15 14 13 12 11 10 9 8 7 6 5 4 3 2 1

With great honor
for
Gene & Gwen Zacharias,
Wycliffe missionaries,
for investing your hands and your feet.

★ ★ ★

CONTENTS

Oh Lord, won't you buy me a Mercedes Benz?
My friends all drive Porsches, I must make amends.

JANIS JOPLIN

FOREWORD
BY STEVE BROWN

I HAVE NO IDEA WHY KAREN ASKED ME TO WRITE A FOREWORD to this book. Maybe she was drinking. I suppose she could have been tired and wasn't thinking clearly. I'm pretty sure it wasn't drugs. Given Karen's incredibly funny way of looking at the world, it could have been a joke.

I'm just not sure.

I'm a right-wing conservative who is so far to the right that I think Rush Limbaugh is a communist. Karen and I share our love for Jesus and the South, and we like each other, but we probably don't vote the same way or hang out on the same side of political discussions.

Maybe her invitation to write this was a kind of conspiracy. It could be that this was the only way she could get this old cynical preacher to move out of his comfort zone and consider some things conservatives generally (and cynics never) consider.

Do you think?

Well, if that was her purpose, it worked.

Frankly, reading Karen's book made me uncomfortable.

Don't get me wrong. It was sometimes funny and she tells a story about as well as anybody I know. But my laugher was sometimes mixed with tears and her stories got down to the rock-hard place of my arrogance, self-righteousness, and the careless thought that I had God figured.

When I was in college, I memorized Wordsworth's words:

> *The world is too much with us; late and soon,*
> *Getting and spending, we lay waste our powers:*
> *Little we see in Nature that is ours;*
> *We have given our hearts away, a sordid boon!*

I thought of those words while reading this book and winced. "Wincing" is good if God is in the wincing, and God is in this book, reminding us that he may not look like the pictures we've been painting, that he doesn't play our games, and that he is not altogether happy with our definition of his blessing. But there's more. Just when we were "headed for the bridge," Karen reminds us that he loves us anyway.

Wordsworth and Karen both write with hope. Wordsworth wrote:

> *So might I, standing on this pleasant lea,*
> *Have glimpses that would make me less forlorn;*
> *Have sight of Proteus rising from the sea;*
> *Or hear old Triton blow his wreathèd horn.*

The difference between Wordsworth and Karen is that his hope is dead because the gods Proteus and Triton were "made-up" gods. Made-up gods can be whatever you want them to be. The reason our lives are so shallow and empty is because we worshiped with Wordsworth instead of the real God to whom Karen Zacharias would send us.

Sometimes you read a book that makes you feel better because it lauds made-up gods and falsely affirms shallow and ego-centered goals. That kind of "feeling better" doesn't last very long. I've been there and done that.

This book has forced this old cynical preacher to try repenting. Now that — while it can be painful in its doing — creates a freedom and a joy that last a lifetime.

Read this book, do your own repenting, and then, when you sense the joy, rise up and call me blessed for having told you about it.

FOREWORD
BY SUSAN ISAACS

I FIRST MET KAREN SPEARS ZACHARIAS THROUGH THE BURNSIDE Writers Collective, an online magazine started by author Donald Miller as a home for young, progressive Christian writers and thinkers to share their ideas. Boy, was I glad Karen arrived; I was no longer the only woman over forty trying to fit in with a team of hipster optimists who had their whole lives ahead of them.

But while we shared the same values as our young hipster, optimist friends — disillusionment with corporatized Christianity, the prosperity gospel, and the deification of the American Dream — Karen and I had more years living through that disillusionment. (Not to brag, I'd trade experience for youth and optimism any day. The chance for a do-over? You bet.)

But if you live the life of faith long enough you will come to realize that God's wonderful plan for your life doesn't resemble a Pottery Barn catalog. Hopefully you'll also realize that most of what's in that catalog is worthless. But maybe your home group leader's house looks like Pottery Barn, and that cute TV preacher's wife made the cover of *House Beautiful* and she shops at Williams Sonoma. So you wonder if it's just you being bitter.

Still you are haunted by an idea that God's plan for your life is more than a cute spouse and Egyptian cotton sheets. You're still obsessed with finding out what God's kind of wonderful is and wondering if anyone else is.

It's like Richard Dreyfuss in *Close Encounters of the Third Kind*, so obsessed with the image of Devil's Tower in his mind, he mashes his potatoes into an effigy at the dinner table. When he finally gets to Devil's Tower and sees all the people with the same papier-mâché obsession, he realizes he wasn't crazy. He was hearing from on high.

Someone's there, and there's something more.

That's what it was like for me, meeting Karen and reading her work. She, too, is sure that God has more for us than a double-wide trailer or Egyptian cotton sheets. And that's what you'll get in *Will Jesus Buy Me A Double-Wide?*: story after story of people who lived the Pottery Barn life and walked away, or went bankrupt trying, or who never even saw such pretty shiny paper. You'll even read about those hucksters who tried to sell you Egyptian cotton for the price of a trailer's down payment.

No, you're not alone in your nagging suspicion that God's kind of wonderful is something more weighty and difficult than mastering a prayer or a key to success; and that it's more often found among the least of these.

Sometimes it takes a trailer trash queen to remind us.

INTRODUCTION

After Daddy died, Mama paid $6,000 for a single-wide trailer, a 12 x 60. It was the first home our family owned. It had plywood walls so thin you could hear a roach grunt, and the only insulation from the outside elements was a feather pillow clutched down over your head during winter or a cooling rag filled with ice cubes for the sticky nights of a Georgia summer.

We moved that trailer five times in six years. Corner lots in the trailer parks were the most coveted because they usually had the biggest yards. Wealthy people lived in trailers with tip-outs. The very rich lived in double-wides. My friend Karin Paris and her brother lived in a double-wide with their mama. They really had it made — all that space for only three people. We had twice as many people living in a trailer half as big.

While I no longer live in a house balanced on cinder blocks the way I did in my youth, I recognize that almost all of my life's truly meaningful moments took place in a trailer. I had my first kiss in a trailer. I smoked my first and last cigarette in a trailer. I asked Jesus into my heart on bended knee in a trailer. I fell madly in love (several different times) in a trailer. And I gave birth to my firstborn child on my mama's bed in a trailer.

Given my druthers, I'd rather reside in a mansion carved

from marble than a 12 x 60 crafted from aluminum siding. Still, I know without question that God's love for me or his favor toward me is not manifested in whether I live at the end of a dirt road in a trailer or around the emerald bend in a gated community comprised of McMansions. Proof of God's love is not found in the square footage of our homes or the number of cars our garage will hold. God's love is not evident in our net worth at all. It's found in the same place it has always been, at the foot of a rough-hewn and bloodied cross.

Now for those of you raised up reciting the books of the B-I-B-L-E and doing the hand motions to "Deep & Wide," the very suggestion that God's love can best be summed up in a yearly financial statement might appear like some sort of newfangled math. (Maybe it's the exact same math they've been using on Wall Street and in the Securities and Exchange Commission lately.)

But there are a lot of folks prancing around treating the Bible like an algebra book and God like their personal banker. They figure if they can do the equation just right, they'll earn God's approval and he'll hand over the keys to the great vault of heaven. Then that abundant life mentioned in John 10:10 will finally be theirs.

I was reminded of just how skewed our thinking is about an abundant life while roaming through a bookstore in Salt Lake City's airport one afternoon. Every which way I looked were copies of *The Secret* by Rhonda Byrne. I thought that an odd choice for a city that is a mecca for Mormons, but it was an airport bookstore, after all, so they weren't marketing solely to the Joseph Smith crowd.

Still, the book was at the top of the shelf, displayed in all its parchment glory, and people were coming along snatching it up, left and right, like they'd just found a Cadbury Egg on a half-price special two days *before* Easter.

I didn't know much about the book then, but I heard a woman say it helped her understand why she had been able to amass so much success and wealth in her life — she had attracted it all to herself. She had called forth all the goodness of the universe for her own good pleasure, and the universe had responded because it was honoring the power of her good energy, just the way *The Secret* promised it would, because, well, that's the power of the law of attraction, as purported by the book. Its real magic lies in the fact that the law is at work whether we acknowledge its powers or not.

The law allows that the earth turns on its orbit for us. That the sun rises and sets for us. That we are the masters of our universe and anything we want can be ours, be it a mansion in Point Clear, Alabama, or healing from the cancer that threatens our very lives. All we have to do is call forth from the universe all that we desire and then trust the universe to grant us our every wish. Just name it and claim it, babe.

This message is like dog hair — it keeps turning up everywhere. I was listening to my daughter's iPod the other day, and there was Destiny's Child preaching their own version: "If I surround myself with positive things I'll gain prosperity."[1] The lyrics don't even make any sense given "Survivor" is a song about a romantic breakup.

Imagine breaking open your uncle's secret stash of white lightning, pouring it into those little empties of Cracker Barrel syrup your mama's been collecting for a Vacation Bible School craft project, and then setting up a curbside stand and selling Mandy's Magic Elixir for $25 a pop. One burning swallow, a tingly head rush, and a few giddy minutes later, and everybody in the neighborhood is clamoring to your stand, eager to buy anything that makes them feel this goooooodddddd.

Nobody cares if you've duped them in the process. The only thing they care about is how it makes them feel, and well, by golly, it feels dang good to believe that we are the masters of the universe. We like the head rush that comes with being told that we can have anything, anything at all our greedy dark hearts desire. Remember, we are the people who built a nation upon the precepts of health, wealth, and the pursuit of happiness.

This isn't quantum physics, as some of *The Secret*'s adherent's have suggested, or even bottle rocket science. It isn't even good theology. It's just old-fashioned cow pies, newly packaged with glitz and glamour, and fashioned to look like Moon Pies.

The cold truth about *The Secret* is that it's a blazing lie. One that Baptists, Pentecostals, Mormons, atheists, and agnostics have been buying in bulk. As you might suspect, matters of logic can be a challenge for a girl who grew up in a trailer, but cut me some slack here and consider this for a moment: If a person's worldview presupposes this so-called "truth" — that whatever good fortune comes our way is a result of our own calling it forth — then the corollary has to be true as well, doesn't it? That any bad thing that comes our way is our own dang fault.

It's a perfect theology for people with means. We convince ourselves that we deserve prosperity because we've worked hard for it. We deserve it because of our faithfulness to God. We teach our children that we have earned God's good favor and that's why we're so rich, so healthy, so pretty, so smart, and so free to do as we doggone please.

However, it's a terrible theology for the poor and downtrodden. When times get hard it must mean God is put out with us. We've been unfaithful or otherwise not measured up. When we get cancer or lose our jobs or homes, well, it must be that we deserve that too. And if someone in our family dies, well, that must be the result of some really major sinning on somebody's behalf, right?

Or maybe not.

Exactly how does the law of attraction apply to the woman who's been raped or the veteran who is homeless? Or the daughter who grows up fatherless? Did these people somehow invite tragedy into their lives?

I began to ponder these matters as I thought about the suggestion that we have the power to create the life we deserve, whatever in the heck that means. The thing is, we Americans want to believe that God loves us best of all and that all of our nation's riches are the result of our faithfulness to God. We also have a tendency to think that our nation's ills have come about because God has to punish all those people misbehavin'. It's just a heap of hooey served on a silver platter (made in China, by the way).

There are those who'll disagree with me, some vehemently, but I believe that whatever blessings we enjoy may be more the result of good geography than good theology. We just happen to live in a place that for the most part has been spared the sort of droughts and freaks of nature that can decimate a country and a people for decades to come. Let an event like Katrina unfold and you get some idea of just how badly things could turn for all of us, in an instant.

If I ruled the world I'd order every single person who bought *The Secret* with the intent to build their wealth to spend a day in downtown Raleigh with the homeless the way I did one Sunday afternoon. Or better yet, I'd march them off to the Union Rescue Mission in Los Angeles to hang with Larry Wilson for a day.

Larry has had a lot more contact with the homeless than I have. I asked Larry to elaborate on what kinds of misconceptions exist about the homeless. Here are Larry's observations:

- *People who are homeless are not spiritual.*

  In fact, most of the homeless people I've met are among the most spiritual people I know. They know what evil is because they've faced it in themselves and on the streets. And they know what faith and hope are, because that's all they have and the power of that keeps them alive. And the ones who survive truly understand the power of Christ's resurrection, because they've experienced it in their own lives. As far as I'm concerned, the people I've met who have endured homelessness know more about life and the power of God than I'll ever know.

- *People who are homeless are all addicts or mentally ill. Or it's their own fault.*

  Just over the past few months, I've met a former screen-writer, a professional photographer who used to work with Annie Liebowitz, a middle-class businessman planning a missionary venture to Uganda (with a wife and child), two elderly women who lost their home to a swindler, an eighty-five-year-old former preacher who ended up penniless and sleeping in the bus station.

  None of them had drug or alcohol problems or mental illness. Increasing numbers of the homeless are middle-class men, women, and families without a safety net — so when they lost jobs and homes, they ended up on Skid Row. Last year at this time, the Union Rescue Mission (whom I work with a lot) was housing 15 families. This year they're housing 59 families, with 200 kids, and they are helping 79 more families with hotel vouchers to keep them off the streets.

- *Homeless people live on the streets.*

  The vast majority of people who are homeless live with friends or family before landing on the streets or in homeless shelters.

- *Homeless people are criminals.*

  I've met many people at Union Rescue Mission with jail records but I've met many, many more who have no criminal past.

- *The homeless are single.*

  Hundreds of two-parent families and single-parent families are homeless in L.A.

- *People who are homeless are self-absorbed "losers" and "loners."*

  The homeless people I've met know more about community and watching out for one another than most of the people I've met in church. They have to watch out for each. They take care of the newly homeless, making sure they know what to do and how to take care of themselves, where the services are, that kind of thing. They share their food. And many are among the most polite people I know.

If Larry wore a hat, it would be a white one. He's what my kin always referred to as "good people." His observations confirm what we all fear but few ever articulate — that the homeless aren't homeless because they've blocked money from coming to them through the power of negative thinking any more than the rich are rich because they summoned their wealth from the great ATM in the Sky.

It's probably a good thing I don't rule the world. I don't even understand it most of the time. I may not be able to explain quantum physics to you but I know one thing for dang sure — we are not masters of our own universe. There is no such thing as the law of attraction. That's not the sort of message that's likely to land me a seat on the yellow couch or a first-pick in Ms. O's book club, but it's the truth, plain as I can tell it.

But I don't expect you to take my word for it. The blessing of being the kind of gal who asks a lot of questions is that nobody really expects me to have any answers. They just expect me to track down the folks who might know a thing or two about these matters. So that's what I've attempted to do here. I've sought out people, some of them complete and utter strangers, and poked my nose into their personal affairs by asking them questions about matters a polite person is never supposed to ask questions about — God and money.

Sometimes I didn't ask questions at all. There were a few times when I just observed people in their daily goings-on. That's the job of a writer, after all, to pay attention. Close attention. You can tell a lot about a person and what's truly important to them just by watching them go about their daily living, or dying, as the case may be.

Specifically, I wanted to know how prosperity, or the lack thereof, affected their faith journey. What did they think about this notion of a Cash & Cadillac Gospel that equates the entire world as one cosmic Super-Mart and life into nothing more than an extravagant consumer excursion?

It is not my intent to widen the already looming abyss between the haves and the have-nots. Greed is not a respecter of people. It threatens all of us, regardless of how many plasma TVs we may or may not have.

Having been there, I can tell you, there's nothing intrinsically good about poverty. It can, and often does, create a good deal of strife among families, communities, and nations. There are a lot of ills associated with poverty — increased rates of domestic abuse, child abuse, alcoholism, drug use, teen pregnancy, and illiteracy, to name a few. God forbid that I do what so many other authors have done and romanticize poverty. There's nothing romantic about having to hitch a ride to work because your car broke down and you can't afford to get it fixed, and the nearest bus stop is two miles out yonder.

As the proud owner of a very fine running BMW myself, I know that the tiniest amount of wealth can inoculate a person to the daily struggle for survival. But having money does not immunize a person from compassion. There are plenty of people, Christian and otherwise, who are using their means to create a better world for a whole host of people. Bono comes to mind. Bill and Melinda Gates. Truett Cathy. Oprah. Rick Warren.

Listen, I wouldn't be here writing on this laptop today if it weren't for the graciousness of friends and strangers alike. Hospitable people I barely know have given me a cabin in the woods to write, or loaned me a truck when I needed it, or put me up for the night and put out lavish spreads of food for nourishment. We live in a nation full of good-hearted people, people eager to help. Between the pages of this book, you'll have the privilege, as I did, to meet some of them.

I've tried to cut a wide swath, interviewing the very wealthy, people like Sister Schubert who sold her Parker House roll business for a whopping $40 million, and those living in poverty, like Miz Betty who never imagined as a young woman that she'd spend her retirement years living in a van in downtown Raleigh. Some of the people I know personally, like the Missionary, and others, like the Ambassador, I met through random introductions.

I intended this book to show my silly side. "But I am really funny!" I told my editor one day after I'd finished up a couple of serious books, one about war and another about murder. "Yes, you are," my editor agreed as he set about pitching this book.

In essence it would be a book crafted by a girl who'd grown up in a trailer house standing on her tiptoes on a rusty bucket peeking into the Pella windows at the lifestyles of the rich-and-wannabes. But I barely got a glimpse of Jesus-bling before the bottom of the bucket gave way, and what had started out as tongue-in-cheek, all of sudden turned very serious as our nation's economy took a very bad tumble and people started losing their jobs (me included), their health care, their 401(k)s, their homes, their cars, and their hope. There's not much funny about losing your health care when you're fighting for your life as the Redhead has been doing.

One of these days I am going to write a book for no other purpose than to give you a good old belly laugh. If it hadn't been for that knot-head Bernie Madoff and those bloats at AIG this might be that book. Not that this is void of hilarity. If you can read the story of the Ambassador without falling over slap-happy or crossing your legs to keep from wetting yourself, you have better bladder control than me, that's for sure. I've never interviewed a more genuine soul than the Ambassador.

He's the reason I do what I do. Writing allows me the opportunity to ask the obvious question — What happened to your fingers? — that I'd probably be too busy to ask if I worked at

Dairy Queen. As my buddy Jack Pendarvis once told me — "I may not be rich, but I lead a rich life."

There is a huge difference between the two and I hope the stories in this book will help you see that. So whether you live in the double-wide or in the van downtown or behind gilded gates of your own choosing, my prayer for you is that you lead a rich life and that you, too, will use your gifts, material or otherwise, to be an Ambassador for Christ.

But hold up just a second, or as the Ambassador says, put your finger there, we'll come back to that. Before I began tracking down all these folks and prying into their lives, I stumbled across an author purporting another version of the name-it-and-claim-it message offered in *The Secret*. This one invoked the name of Christ but basically promised the same material rewards, and buddy, I'm here to tell you, there's a built-in audience for golden-calf theology here in America.

THE EVANGELIST

A GAZILLION PEOPLE LINED UP ON A SUNNY SPRING DAY, THE kind of day best spent lounging poolside, to have a television evangelist autograph copies of her latest book. She's reportedly authored sixty such books.

The Evangelist lives like the celebrity she is, in a multimillion-dollar parsonage. She has a multimillion-dollar corporate jet at her disposal and a hairdresser who sometimes travels with her. The Evangelist does not apologize for her lavish lifestyle. She believes that as a child of God she's entitled to it.

The attraction to the finer things of life is only natural, says the Evangelist: "Who would want to get in on something where you're miserable, poor, broke and ugly and you just have to muddle through until you get to heaven?" she asks. "I believe God wants to give us nice things."[1]

A sign posted at the bookstore stated that there would be no "personal autographs." The Evangelist would sign her signature only. I mused over what author and historian Shelby Foote would think of all this hoopla. Foote reportedly refused to autograph books for anyone but friends. He said friends were the only ones his signature meant anything to. Rumor circulating among the frenzied crowd waiting on the Evangelist claimed

1,300 people had waited in line in Birmingham the day before. There were seven hundred-plus on that day.

Event planners had roped off Church Street in Fairhope, Alabama, and set up a stage. They had dancers, singers, and a praise and worship band. I was new to town and unaccustomed to celebrities of any sort. I'd grabbed a latte at the coffee shop and was sitting outside at a table, reading, when a sweet-faced woman with a halo of white hair asked if she could join me. Why sure, I said.

Her name was Evelyn. She was eighty-five but didn't look a day over seventy. She said she and her daughter had driven over two hours for the chance to get a glimpse and a signature from the guest author.

Evelyn didn't look like the sort of person who reads *Rolling Stone* or *People* magazine, consuming celebrity culture. She seemed to be the real sensible sort, so I asked her why she went to all that effort for this event.

"I tune in to her television show every morning," Evelyn said about the Evangelist. "She teaches the Scriptures but she talks plainly." Evelyn said that sometimes the Evangelist could sound like an upset schoolmarm, but Evelyn found that charming in an old-fashioned sort of way.

Evelyn didn't suppose she was actually going to read the autographed book that her daughter and hundreds of others were standing in line for. No need to, really, she already knew the woman's story from watching her television program every morning.

The Evangelist had grown up in an abusive home with an alcoholic father. That alone provided her with an immediate audience. Experts estimate that one in five children grow up in homes with an alcoholic parent. Evelyn said she thought many people could relate to all that this Evangelist had been through.

I wasn't sure if Evelyn knew about the U.S. Senate's investigation into the Evangelist's financial affairs, but I decided not to mention it. The Evangelist was only one of several high-profile celebrity evangelists whose financial shenanigans had drawn the attention of Republican Sen. Chuck Grassley of Iowa, a member of the Committee on Finance. Grassley called for an accounting of expenses, executive compensation and perks, gifts, etc. Because these ministries are run as church-based nonprofits, they aren't held to the same accountability and oversight as other corporations.[2]

When Grassley made his request some of the ministries balked at it. Some called in their own chariots of accountants and attorneys. They decried that this was a violation of the separation of church and state law. To her credit, the Evangelist has been cooperating with Grassley's investigation. In the wake of the current recession, she's even scaled back her lavish lifestyle, put some of those mansions of hers up for sale.

As I studied all those women snaking down Church Street, I wondered if they had read Grassley's reports. Did they know that the homes, bought and paid for by the ministry, were valued in the millions? Moreover, I wondered, does it matter to them? Or did they just see all that wealth of hers as proof of God's adoration of the Evangelist?

The Evangelist touts a prosperity message: God wants to bless us. He wants to pour out his goodness upon us. He wants us to lead a life more abundant, specifically, a life filled with more creature comforts.

I was befuddled because Evelyn didn't seem to be the sort of person who cared much about money. In fact, she told me as much herself. Evelyn lives in a part of Mississippi that was hard-hit by Hurricane Katrina. Her home was fine, but her son and his family, they lost everything. Every bead board of their home was destroyed. They moved in with her until they got their FEMA trailer. They'd lived in it for nearly two years and had only recently moved into a new home.

Evelyn lifted her glasses and wiped the tears from her eyes as she told me how thankful she was that her family had all survived the storm. That wasn't the case for some in her town.

"I'm sorry," she said, apologizing for her tears.

"Don't be," I replied. "If these things aren't worth crying over, what is?"

As her daughter inched up in the line, Evelyn took leave to join her. I sat alone at the table until well after dark, enjoying the music and marveling at the multitudes. When the last of the books had been signed, around ten p.m., the Evangelist walked through the coffee shop crowd, her entourage following like obedient children. Dozens of people, who had not stood in line for her autograph, still pressed their noses up against the windowpanes, trying to get a glimpse of the Celebrity Evangelist. I wondered if it was because we are all hungry to be part of something special or if it's because we're all so sick we need to touch the hem of one that has the power to heal.

★

This notion that God wants to prosper us isn't a new one. Its roots are most often traced back to the emergence of the postwar middle class, and a couple of evangelists, Oral Roberts and Kenneth Hagin. Television played a huge part in getting their version of the Cadillac Gospel before an emerging middle class.

"What Oral did was develop a theology that made it okay

to prosper," said David Harrell Jr.. Harrell is a former Eminent Scholar at Auburn University in Auburn, Alabama, and Roberts' biographer. "Roberts let Pentecostals be faithful to the old-time truths their grandparents embraced and be part of the modern world, where they could have good jobs and make money."[3]

This "name-it-and-claim-it" brand of Christianity is preached in various denominations today, although it's most often attributed to Pentecostal or charismatic churches. Believers are encouraged to tithe and then some, with the insinuation, if not outright promise, that God will return to them tenfold, or abundantly beyond all measure.

Rev. Otis Moss of Trinity United Church of Christ in Chicago says that such a theology is more focused on making money than it is about religion.

"Televangelists are presenting a prosperity gospel where they are promoting a Jesus that is more like a cosmic bellhop, versus a Christ who is engaging in the current issues," Moss said.[4]

No question about it, the Jesus-factor is a great selling point for everything from bobble-head dolls to theme parks to presidential bids. Senator John McCain was shuffling through an anemic race for the nation's highest office in 2008 until some savvy marketing team saw the light and yanked then Alaska Governor Sarah Palin up to the podium. Once McCain enlisted help from the Lord's Army — Palin is a Pentecostal — his value rose significantly among the evangelical ranks. That Jesus-factor momentarily locked McCain into a dead-heat with Senator Barack Obama.

More importantly, within hours after McCain introduced his running mate, the Republican National Convention took in $1 million in donations, most of that flowing in over the internet.[5] Sure enough, when it comes to the power of media marketing, the name of Jesus is a better brand than Coca-Cola, Aflac, and Nike combined.

★

I once read a book written by a man with Dr. in front of his name, who claimed that God nudged him awake in the middle of the night and spoke audibly to him. I don't know about you, but if God woke me in the middle of the night for a chitchat, I'd probably die of fright. Surely God of all people knows better than to disturb a woman in her sleep, right?

But this fellow said he woke straight up and heard God clearly speak Proverbs 3:5–6 over him: *Trust in the Lord with all your heart and lean not on your own understanding. In all your ways acknowledge Him, and He shall direct your paths* (NKJV).

(How odd. God has apparently grown so accustomed to us doing it that he refers to himself in the third person. He's like a lawyer that way, I guess.)

Or, if you buy into this man's theology, more like a financial advisor. During his brief encounter with a chatty nocturnal Creator, this man said he learned the perfect will of God for each and every one of us: Get saved. Live right. Build the kingdom. Prosper.[6] And we should dress well while we go about it. The good author points to Scripture to make his point that "It would seem that God doesn't want us to look weird. He wants us to look better than everyone else."[7]

> *Your cheeks are beautiful with earrings,*
> *your neck with strings of jewels.*
> *We will make you earrings of gold,*
> *studded with silver.*
> Song of Solomon 1:10–11

Dolly Parton might want to rethink that image of hers. As she so often says, "It takes a lot of money to look this cheap." If this fellow is right, God doesn't shop at Walmart. It seems God is the sort of man who knows the personal shopper at Nordstrom on a first-name basis.

Who knew Christ was so class-conscious? This fellow suggested that Jesus purposely surrounded himself with people who could help finance his ministry: "The people Jesus called to follow him were people who were working or wealthy."[8] And contrary to popular notion, so says this author, Jesus wasn't a poor man. "He could attract the rich to him primarily because he was rich himself."[9]

All part of that "takes-one-to-know-one" discipleship approach, I guess. To be fair, these quotes are lifted out of a nearly two-hundred-page book, so, yes, they are out-of-context, but the bulk of that content is built upon the thesis that God's good pleasure for us amounts to us being rich, very, very rich. Millionaires, in fact.

This is golden-calf theology personified.

It brings to mind an image from David Sedaris's book, *Dress Your Family in Corduroy and Denim*.

Sedaris tells of the night the Tomkeys, their neighbors, came trick-or-treating, the night *after* Halloween. His mother had already given out all the candy. The only household sweets that remained was what the Sedaris children had gathered the night before. Mrs. Sedaris instructed her children to grab some of the candy from their bags to share with the Tomkey kids.

Being children and all, they weren't inclined to share. Instead Sedaris dumped his candy on the bed and began to rip through the miniature chocolate bars, stuffing his face. When his mother showed up, aiming to collect the candy herself,

Sedaris lunged for the pile and tore through it in an effort to keep his mother from giving out even the least favored sweets. "These were the second-best things I had received, and while it hurt to destroy them, it would have hurt more to give them away," Sedaris later recalled.

Finally, as a bit of remorse began to settle in, Sedaris began to see himself as his mother may have seen him: "Here is a boy sitting on a bed, his mouth smeared with chocolate. He's a human being, but also he's a pig, surrounded by trash and gorging himself so that others may be denied."[10]

I wonder if that is the image of us that comes to God's mind whenever we go around boasting that it is his Sovereign will that all God's children be rich.

THE SISTER

Sister Schubert makes dough, literally and figuratively.
Go to the freezer section of near about any chain grocery store and you're sure to find her rolls. They're smacking good too. Sister says they may not be the best rolls you've ever eaten — your granny's might be better — but they'll be the best you've ever bought.

"Try these," she says, placing a paper plate laden with steaming sausage rolls on a table top.

Her real name is Patricia Barnes, but she offers, "Everyone calls me Sister."

She doesn't much favor that ornate gold-framed portrait of her decked out in a beaded ball gown that hangs in the entry to her Luverne, Alabama, factory. Instead, she prefers a white lab coat, which she's wearing today over her black slacks, as she runs around her office in her stocking feet.

Sister is not a froufrou kind of gal, which is not to say she isn't pretty — she is, but in a tomboyish way. She's got the slim, petite build of an eighth-grade cheerleader and the effervescent spirit to match. If she ever had a pretentious bone she must've thrown it out back for the yard dogs to devour.

Her office is nicely appointed with the customary expansive

dark-wood desk that you would expect from the corporate head of a multimillion-dollar business. There are shiny crystal lamps on the end tables and glossy framed articles from *Bon Appetit* and *Southern Living* magazines hanging on the walls. Guests are offered a seat in the upholstered chairs while Sister pulls up a rocker. She calls it her "Come talk to Mama" chair. It's a lot less intimidating for employees to talk to the boss who sits in a rocker, than the boss woman who sits behind the big desk, she explains.

Situated out a ways from the big city of Troy, Alabama, Luverne bills itself as the friendliest city in the South. There's a cash & carry, a hardware store, a couple of poultry producers, and some timber folks, but this factory that houses Sister Schubert's Homemade Rolls is the town's largest employer.

"Every single one of our rolls is placed into the pan by hand," Sister says, proudly.

The company handles a lot of dough, about $60 million a year in nationwide sales.

Not far from the rocker where Sister sits is a tell-tale red wagon filled with toys, trains and trucks, mostly. Toys for Alex, the boy Sister adopted from the Ukraine. She made her first trip to the country in 2003.

"People ask me how it is I picked Ukraine," says Sister. "I didn't. God showed it to me."

Actually, it was a missionary couple speaking at a Luverne Rotary meeting who first introduced Sister to the Ukraine. As she listened to their tale, Sister felt an unfamiliar stirring. Something moving her beyond the borders of her beloved Alabama. She had to go, had to see this place of which they spoke.

★

Sister had always known that God would use her in a big way. Her father had prophesied it when she was only twelve. "Daddy told me, 'You've been blessed but you're going to be given great responsibility. You'll take care of your family and other people.'"

Boy, did that prophecy ever come true, but in all the unexpected heartbreaking ways that young girls and their daddies can never imagine. At age forty, Sister was faced with a marriage that was ending badly.

Seventeen years prior she'd been a junior, studying interior design, when she dropped out of Auburn University to become a Delta Air Lines stewardess. She met her first husband during her preliminary training course in Houston. He was charming and all things wonderful. After three dates, Sister knew she would marry him. But what a twenty-year-old finds charming often becomes wearisome once children and responsibility arrive. The marriage unraveled. There's nothing to be gained by speaking ill of an ex, so Sister prefers to just leave it at that.

Her daddy's prophecy that she was going to have to take care of her family was never more obvious than after the divorce. There were two daughters, twelve and sixteen, to provide for, to see through college; how was she going to manage all that? Sister had abandoned her career path long ago. Sure, she had a bit of a business sense about her, skills she'd picked up working at her family's furniture business over the years. But how was she going to parlay those skills into a living wage?

Like most southern women, Sister came from a long line of people who liked to eat, and ever since her toddler hands could palm a wooden spoon, Sister loved to cook. Her recipe file was full of batter-stained hand-me-downs. Grandmothers, aunts from both sides of the family, as well as her own mother, were all terrific cooks and they'd been generous to share their favorite recipes with her.

There was one in particular that had earned Sister favored status among the church crowd at St. Mark's Episcopal in Troy, Alabama. It was the Parker House rolls she made for the holiday fair. She'd made twenty pans of frozen rolls and donated them to sell that first year. The next year the fair folks asked if she could make two hundred pans. In 1991, they asked her for three hundred.

Sister figured if the folks at St. Mark's liked them so much, maybe others would too. So she approached a supermarket in Troy and asked the manager if he would be interested in carrying her rolls. They said they'd give it a shot. From that first day, Sister says, "I felt like God was saying, 'I'm with you. I'll help you.'"

Boy, howdy. Has he ever been faithful to honor that.

"God's the best business partner there is," says Sister.

Ask any marketing person, they'll tell you that the best form of advertising for any product is word of mouth. Sister had the good sense to plop warm yummy yeast rolls in the mouths of hundreds who then went forward to testify to thousands that her rolls were indeed the best on the market.

The business that had started in her home and branched out to one of her daddy's warehouses expanded to the showplace facility made possible by the forward-thinking people in Luverne who begged her to bring her business to their town, to employ their people. Less than a decade after she took her first batch of rolls to the supermarket, Sister Schubert's Homemade Rolls was sold to Lancaster Colony Corp. of Ohio. Sister received a $40 million return on her investment of prayers, sweat, and flour. She calls it her first Cinderella story. Another would follow.

★

Forty-million is a lot of smack. A girl could buy some serious bling with that kind of cash. She could have a walk-in closet stuffed full of Jimmy Choos. But the truth is, Sister had no idea what to do with all that dough.

"I asked God, why did you trust me with all this money? I'm just a little bitty person," Sister says.

Prior to selling her business, Sister equated a $100,000 annual salary with success. She didn't have a clue how to manage $40 million.

People who come into a lot of money learn quickly that they also come into a lot of friends they never knew they had before, and more than a few long-lost relatives. People were continually on Sister's doorstep with their hands out for one cause or another.

"It's hard to tell them no," she says. "Sometimes I've gotten angry when I know it's not right for them to be asking what they are asking for. I've learned to go to God. He's always given me wise counsel to deal with the situation."

Money should be a vehicle, not a destination. Sister believed that if the money was hers, it was hers for a reason, a reason beyond sheer provision for herself and her children.

"I don't think God cares whether we are wealthy or not, but I think he does care that we do the right thing with whatever he's given us."

She admits that she hasn't always done the right thing. Tithing's a no-brainer when you don't have much money. It's easier to give $500 on the $5000 she'd earned than $500,000 of the $5 million, Sister says. The more money she made, the less percentage she gave.

"He blessed us with so much," she says, yet she struggled to give back. "As I made more, I went from giving my 10 percent to giving only 5 percent."

Sister shakes her head in a disbelieving way, as if she can hardly comprehend what's coming out of her own mouth. It makes so little sense, she admits. Call it the law of affluence. The more money one has the greater the greed temptation.

She's working her way back into proper giving.

"I learned a lesson, and I'm back to giving where I should be," she says.

That first year, in 2001, Sister lost $2 million of her $40 million in the dot com market. It made her physically ill to lose so much money. She couldn't understand why God would trust her with so much when she knew so little about investing it. Sister couldn't stand the idea of losing that much money ever again. Impulsively, she blurted out to God that she'd rather just give it all away than lose it.

When she first started making rolls, Sister wanted to find a way to help the hungry of the world. Recalling that desire, Sister started the Barnes Family Foundation. The Foundation would enable her to fulfill that vision in ways she couldn't even begin to imagine.

★

The children at Sasha's Home do not know Sister as the famous baker woman. Their name for her is Sister Mama. She is the woman who provided them with the cheerful home where they live with their foster parents as they await adoption into a forever family.

When Sister made her first trip to the Ukraine her mission was pretty straightforward. She wanted to visit the Abandoned

Baby Center in Gorlovoka. She was not prepared for what she would encounter.

At that time in the Ukraine, orphaned or abandoned children were being turned over to the nearest state-run facility, even if that facility happened to be a prison. In Gorlovoka it was a hospital. Healthy babies were housed along with sick babies. The state-run orphanages were full of children but they had very little in the way of supplies or staffing. Babies received one bottle a day and two diaper changes, one in the morning and one at night.

There was never enough staff to love on them, to rock them and sing them lullabies. Babies sprawled in their cribs listlessly, their eyes vacant. Children with any sort of physical impairment, be it club feet or crossed eyes, had no future hope of being adopted. They would be turned out to the streets to become beggars.

The missionary couple Sister met at Rotary asked local officials if they could have a wing in the hospital. They would then staff and maintain the wing to care for the healthy babies. Churches supplied the couple with clothing, diapers, bottles, all the things babies and toddlers need. Sister became a partner in that ministry.

On her second trip in 2004, as they were transporting ten babies, Sister noticed a nurse and translator talking. Both women had tears in their eyes. When Sister asked what they were talking about, they told her about one little boy whose mother had been murdered and whose father had not come forward. The toddler had club feet, a condition that would relegate him to a beggar's life.

Sister noticed the towheaded cherub with the big green eyes the moment she walked into the room lined with cribs. Slowly she approached his crib. The tyke reached out his fingers for hers. It was, Sister recalled, as if he were asking, "Are you the one? Are you the one who is going to save me?"

It would take nearly two years from that day, but Sister did save the toddler from a life on the streets by making sure he got surgery to repair his feet. She also made sure he was adopted into a forever family — hers.

Aware that there were dozens of children just like her new son, Alex, Sister began to cast around for a more permanent home for those children. She found a kindergarten site that had been built during Stalin's reign. It was the typical government-construct, a cement block building painted the grey of despair.

Sister bought it and set about transforming that site. There would be a total of eight apartments, each with five bedrooms, where sixty-four children could be cared for by local foster parents. It might not be their forever home but it would be a place where they could be part of a family.

Launching Sasha's Home took years of working in concert with government officials and local craftsmen. *Sasha* is the Ukrainian nickname for *Alex*. Sister wanted to paint the building yellow, something that would reflect the warmth and love she felt for these children. Locals told her she would never get approval to paint any building in the Ukraine such a bold color, but she did.

"You come around a corner and that house beams sunshine to me," Sister says.

She also added a smaller apartment so that couples looking to adopt a child would have a place to stay. It gives them the opportunity to interact with children they are considering adopting.

The vision God gave to Sister for these children became

infectious. Her hairdresser back in Alabama held a fundraiser to buy mosquito netting for the children's beds. A furniture store in Andalusia, Alabama, provided all the furnishings for the apartments. Several cargo boxes filled with dressers and beds and chairs left Mobile Bay the same week that Russia invaded Georgia in 2008.

"We had no idea if that furniture would arrive or not," Sister says. She did the only thing she knew to do — she prayed: "God, it's in your hands."

Six weeks passed and yet no furniture arrived. Sister and the staff had pretty much given up hope of any furnishings reaching Sasha's Home when the cargo arrived.

"You should have seen everyone, rubbing their hands over those dressers, crying, as if this were the finest furniture ever made. You'd have to go there to understand what they experienced," Sister says. "It was unbelievable."

Sister has had the good fortune to see how generous Americans can be when they set their pocketbooks and minds to it.

"We hear a lot about greed, and there are greedy people in America, but we are also the most giving people on earth," Sister says. "Despite the economically challenging times I do not see that stopping."

When she first started funneling the million-plus it took to build Sasha's Home, Sister worried. Would she lose that money the same as she had when she invested in the dot com market?

"But I feel really good about that now," Sister says. "This money is an investment in the children of the Ukraine. It is being used the way God intended. The blessing of it all has returned to me tenfold."

Just not necessarily in dollars and dimes.

People used to tell Sister that the story of her rolls was like a Cinderella story come true.

"I've had two Cinderella stories," Sister says. "Two truly amazing dreams come true."

Following the opening of Sasha's Home, the Ukraine government bestowed upon Sister one of their country's highest award for humanitarian actions. Her work in the Ukraine has brought meaning to her life in a way that wealth alone never could.

"I realize that there are so many people out there for whom money is everything. It's all they see. It's all they focus on. They worry that they've lost 60 percent of their stocks. Yet, they still have more money than they could spend to live very comfortably."

But Sister has learned that happiness doesn't come from money. It comes from having something to do that makes your life worthwhile. She points to the caretaker at Sasha's Home as an example.

"He feeds the birds, waters the plants, and fixes all the doll strollers, and he's happy doing that. Happiness is about living every day fulfilled and loving what you do."

Sasha's Home is all about being the change Sister wanted to see in the world. Funds from her own recipe book, Cast Your Bread Upon the Waters (castyourbreaduponthewaters.com), have been designated to help perpetuate the work of Sasha's Home.

As she reflected on the gifts the Ukrainian children have given her, Sister implemented a new rule for her own family.

"We no longer say, 'I wish I had' or 'I want' anymore. We are learning to be thankful for what we have every day. If God only gives me the gift of this day and nothing else, I will thank him for that too."

Sister recently came across that roll recipe that her grandmother stuck in a cookbook some eighty years ago. The name ascribed to her family's favorite was "Everlasting Rolls."

"My grandmother knew long before I did that these rolls would have an everlasting mark on this world."

THE CHILDREN

MENTION THE NAME OF MARJOE TO ANYONE WHO CAME OF age during the advent of television and they are likely to recall the curly-headed child who gained notoriety as the nation's youngest evangelist. Marjoe — a derivative of Mary and Joseph — became an ordained preacher at the age of four.

His parents claimed that Marjoe received a vision while taking a bath and so they began to train him in the ways of the Lord and RCA (Radio Corporation of America). His mother was a flamboyant evangelist herself, with a keen eye for the camera. She spent hours drilling him on the sermons he was forced to memorize.

"As a child, I would want to go out and play but we would spend hours and hours memorizing. My mind would begin to slip and finally my mother would lose her patience with me. She would put a pillow over my head and smother me for a little bit or hold me under a water faucet. But she would never put any marks on my body because she knew I would have to be before the press. So she never hit me or anything."[1]

In a white suit that matched her son's, Marjoe's mother would smile at the camera as she introduced the then eight-year-old evangelist: "All across the nation for the past four years, the little preacher has been going up and down, winning lost humanity with the message of the Master."[2]

Behind every message from the Master, however, was one from the boy's mother. Coded messages designed to manipulate the audience. Whenever he said the word *Jesus*, Marjoe had been coached to open his arms wide. If he said *Devil*, he had to step forward. If his mother or father happened to shout out "Glory to God," Marjoe knew the real message was "Speed it up, bud." And if his mother hollered out "Praise God," what she really meant was, "You've got the people where you need them — better take an offering now."[3]

For his part, Marjoe enjoyed all the attention and adoration of adults twice as big as him. But he did not, at any point, believe in any of it. How could he? He'd been taught that the message of Christ was designed for one purpose — to manipulate the masses so that they would reach deep into their pocketbooks and give up dollars by the fistful. Marjoe estimated that by the time he was sixteen, his parents had made $3 million from his preaching.

"I can't think of a time when I believed in God. Or I thought it was a miracle of God that I preached. I knew I could do it well. My parents had trained me. But I never thought I was some miracle child of any kind," he said.[4]

Sadly Marjoe wasn't the last child evangelist to attract the masses.

★

Todd Durham Sr. has been keeping track of how much money Christian evangelist Joel Osteen makes. "Joel is at $76 million a year," he says.[5]

There's a reason this Florida father is closely following what's happening at the big stadium in Texas. "One day I'm hoping that Terry will be at about $86 million."[6]

Eleven-year-old Terry is one of Todd Durham's twin boys. Terry was six years old when he became an ordained minister, thanks to his grandmother Sharon Monroe, who founded True Gospel Deliverance Ministry, a nondenominational church in Fort Lauderdale, the church that ordained Terry.

Todd Durham serves as his young son's promoter. Billed as the "Little Man of God," Sharon Monroe claims her grandson can heal people. Speaking to an ABC News crew, Monroe said she's seen the lame rise up after a healing touch from Terry.

"I've seen peoples being healed, I've seen peoples being delivered, I've seen peoples come in their wheelchairs and walk," Monroe said. "I've seen peoples come in with their cane and put their cane down, I've seen people come in their crutches, lay the crutches down."[7]

She's also seen Terry's ministry grow into a fledgling empire. There are dozens and dozens of speaking engagements. There's an always evolving website (www.ministerterrydurham.org). The site that used to offer T-shirts and the promise of hats and bags to come has been scaled back. Perhaps in reaction to some of the negative publicity that has surfaced as Terry's profile climbs.

But there's no question as to Todd Durham's intent for his son.

"I see Terry Durham as a major icon for the Christian industry," he told ABC News. "Jesus is the product."[8]

Terry's promoters — primarily his father and his grandmother — compare him to the likes of the Reverend Martin Luther King Jr. and Al Sharpton. They have groomed him for the job and they serve on the board that oversees his ministry. That board is compromised of Terry, his father, and his grandmother.

Sharon Monroe doesn't hesitate to upbraid her grandson if he fails to conduct himself properly from the pulpit. She will chide him about his failure to close the service with a proper prayer or about his willfulness. She orders him to prepare for his sermons in much the same fashion as a parent ordering their child to complete their homework.

For Monroe, it's all part of training up a child in the way they should go.

"Terry Durham was chosen by God to let people know that his Spirit lives," she said.[9]

For his part, Terry likes the attention he gets from speaking in as many as a dozen events a week. He's preached in thirty-seven states and in five countries. And, even though he doesn't charge a speaking fee, he's making money hand-over-fist. As much as five thousand dollars is collected in love offerings for one engagement.

Neither his father nor his grandmother will comment on just how much money Terry has made, but his father insists that a portion of it goes into a trust fund for Terry and his twin brother. The rest of the balance goes toward paying promotional expenses, those items managed by his father. Travel and food, lodging and shopping sprees to the mall. Terry likes to dress matchy-matchy from his head to his toes.

Terry believes he has been called by God to preach, although he admits, sometimes it's difficult to differentiate God's voice from his own thoughts. Or maybe from the thoughts of those who are planting the seeds of manipulation in the young boy's life.

In May, 2009, reporters for ABC News discovered that Terry's father and his grandmother both had criminal records. After his son was born, Todd Durham Sr. was convicted on weapons charges and served nearly three years in prison on drug charges. In 2000, Terry's grandmother was convicted of grand theft and organized fraud for her part in a phony sweepstakes operation that targeted the elderly. She served three years probation.[10]

Thrusting a child into the pulpit's limelight, all the while declaring that he has an anointing from God, is just plain abusive. It reveals a real lack of integrity on somebody's behalf. But that compulsion that motivates others to exploit children in this fashion exists in all of us. Underlying it is a belief that we have a special anointing that others have been denied. We couch our specialness in patriotic remarks that border on nationalism: America is a nation blessed by God. God has poured out his favor on America. We are a Christian nation. Our president is a Christian man.

The very way we frame our drummed-up gratitude makes it clear to the rest of the world that God loves America best. How else can you explain all the ways in which he has indulged us? We have more toys, better homes, faster cars, the best schools, bigger bank accounts, and enough firepower to make the gatekeepers of hell envious.

We might never be so crass as to attach a numerical value to our devotion to God the way Todd Durham Sr. has done, but our theology isn't much different than his. We're just more covert about it.

Many of us have this notion that God owes us better than we've gotten. Why else would we wait in line for hours, buying books about the ten steps toward happiness, God's way? We don't expect that the authors of those books are going to tell us to sell everything we own and donate it all to help the poor. Nope. What we expect them to tell us is that God wants to make us rich. That if we just trust him enough, we can have that house on five acres with the four-car garage. If we obey him he's going to give us our heart's desire, which includes that winter house in Sedona, Arizona, and the summer home at Blowing Rock, North Carolina.

We've taken Jeremiah 29:11, *"For I know the plans I have for you," declares the Lord, "plans to prosper you and not to harm you, plans to give you hope and a future,"* and made it into a turnkey verse that guarantees God is going to prosper us, with a multitude of IRAs and investment securities, preferably.

A 2006 *TIME* magazine poll revealed that a whopping 61 percent of those surveyed said that they believed God wants them to be prosperous, and 31 percent said if you give money to God, God will bless you with more money.[11]

In essence, we espouse a Voodoo Christianity — a belief that we can manipulate God.

Osteen, pastor of the 17,000-strong Lakewood megachurch in Houston, has indeed made a significant fortune by promoting such a message. His books are filled with anecdotal stories of how his faith has earned him bigger homes in better neighborhoods, first-class seating on flights, and the best parking spaces, all signs of God's favor upon him.

Not everyone agrees with Osteen's big life under the Jesus tent theology.

The whole idea of God wanting us to be rich is laughable, says Pastor Rick Warren, who heads up Saddleback, another megachurch, this one in Southern California. "This idea that God wants everybody to be wealthy?" he snorts. "There is a word for that: baloney. It's creating a false idol. You don't measure your self-worth by your net worth. I can show you millions of faithful followers of Christ who live in poverty. Why isn't everyone in the church a millionaire?"[12]

But even those of us who shy away from Osteen as he stands before the throngs like some P.T. Barnum of Christianity, choreographing our best lives now, still quietly believe that if we are faithful to God we're going to be rewarded with a pretty good life in the here and now. The prosperity theology we buy into is more insidious than that being offered by TV evangelists. We envision quiet Lake Wobegon lives, "where all the women are strong, all the men are good-looking and all the children are above-average" and all our bills are paid in full.

We Americans are obsessed with obtaining and maintaining a standard of comfort and we like to envision that God is too. Contrast that with the experiences of Christians in other countries. Author Philip Yancey recounts a conversation he had with a man who visits unregistered house churches in China. Yancey asked the man whether Chinese Christians pray against the government's harsh policies. "After thinking for a moment, he replied that not once had he heard a Chinese Christian pray for relief."

"They assume they'll face opposition," Yancey noted. "They can't imagine anything else."[13]

The problem with that sort of Christianity, the kind that expects something other than the good life, is that it is such a hard package to market. All that talk of prisons and the hard life is a downer, dude. Nobody wants to hear about suffering. Besides, negative talk like that makes those folks on Wall Street — the people trying to market that Glitsy, Bejeweled God in which we trust — jittery.

Granted, I wouldn't trust a gussied-up God even if he showed up at my front door with a check from the Publisher's Clearing-House Sweepstakes that he had personally endorsed.

Then again, God probably wouldn't buy time on the early

morning airwaves to get his message across. I doubt he'd even participate in social networking via Twitter or Facebook. I'm pretty sure God would decline an invitation to ride on a float in the Macy's Thanksgiving Day Parade or to make an appearance on the *Colbert Report* (sorry, Stephen). I don't think God is a fan of pop culture at all.

I rather think of God as being more like Shelby Foote, holed up in a room with books somewhere, using a quill pen to journal all of his daily observations. I might be wrong, but I suspect he'd be a lot more comfortable sharing a cup of joe with the man they call the Mayor, than he would be sharing a stage with some boob tube evangelist. And I'm pretty sure God would rip the gonads off anybody who pimped out a child in Jesus' name.

THE MAYOR

A RED DIRT DEVIL VACUUM CLEANER SITS OUT UNDERNEATH the Live Oak. Around the corner weathered shoes, some covered in cobwebs, hang from a metal post. A wad of aluminum in a Ziploc bag, half-filled with water, hangs above the man's head as he sits on his porch, watching television.

"It's an insect repellent," he says, referring to the hanging bag.

That's important information to heed down in swamp territory, where West Nile virus is more than just a story about some other poor fellow — it's a real threat.

The television is tuned to *The Price Is Right*. It's the new version with Drew Carey as host. Carey looks slimmer in black-and-white.

They say the Mayor's kin once built an entire fence out of empty beer cans and whiskey bottles. Now that's the kind of border patrol project that could amuse a person. Mayor wears a white T-shirt and two days' growth of gray stubble. This man who really does live at the end of a dusty red road has hair that is graying now, but he's still lean as the boy he once was, back when he belonged to Uncle Sam.

He joined the Army for no particular reason. Just something to do. Crossed his mind sometime between high school and the future, so he marched down to the recruiting office and gave the fellow there his name and Social Security number in exchange for a one-way ticket to Fort Polk. They said if a boy could survive basic training in Louisiana he'd do just fine in the jungles of Vietnam. That wasn't always the case, but that's the way they told it, and there were some who took it as the gospel.

Lucky for him they quit that war before needing him. He never had to use a gun for anything but killing squirrels. Mayor grew bored with the Army and all that marching and yes-sir, no-sir rigmarole.

"I was looking for a distraction," he says, reasoning that's why he started attending the Bible church in town. "Or maybe I was just searching for an audience."

One thing he's not too clear on was whether he went there looking for Jesus, or if he was much more interested in the girls with the freckled skin, girls with skin white as cotton, and girls with skin brown as bread crust. Girls had long captured the Mayor's interest in a way that matters of the spirit did not.

"Army people bored me. I liked going to church. The people there were good to me," Mayor says.

Mayor is not his name, or a title, but more a designation by default. When you live in the deep woods, you learn to govern yourself and the critters that answer your call.

The men in the church, the fathers of all those pretty girls, took a special liking to this quiet-spoken fellow with the easy smile. He had all the outward appearances of a good Christian man. He held his tongue and wasn't prone to anger. Any drinking he did, he did elsewhere. He was at church nearly every time the doors were open. It hadn't taken Mayor long to figure out that any meal served at church was bound to include fried chicken, done right, and a slice of peach pie. Beat that Army grub all to heck.

After a while, the folks at church asked Mayor if maybe he'd be interested in giving a talk from the pulpit. If he could give a word about all that Jesus had done in his life. So he climbed right up behind that wooden podium, stared out over that congregation of kindly people, then smiled at them with those happy eyes of his and began telling them a story.

He doesn't remember now what he said to them. His recall is sometimes bleary-eyed, the edges of his memory burnt by too much whiskey. But he remembers that those church people liked what he had to say that day because they asked him back again and again.

He accepted their invitations because he was a born storyteller, and they were an attentive audience. The only time they ever interrupted him was to shout out "Amen" or "Say it again." But that wasn't often, since this was a church of white people mostly; their shouting was something they saved for the ballgames.

They say if you really seek after Jesus, he'll be found. Makes a person wonder if life is some kind of cosmic hide-and-go-seek game. Jesus finds the best place to hide and we have to hunt through the darkest of forests to find him. He snickers when we get tripped up. Or when we walk within three inches of him and yet fail to see him, crouching there at our feet.

Mayor never could sort all that out. Why people would waste their lives searching for a God intent on not being found. So he gave it up. Figured life's too short to chase after God when there were women to be had. Women willing to be caught in broad daylight.

That's not exactly the sort of Revelation that the folks at

church wanted to be hearing from Mayor, though, so he did his best to give them the stories they wanted to hear. Love stories of a different sort.

He told them about life in the military and about life in the deep woods. How living underneath oaks as old as this country put matters into perspective for him. He read to them from the wisdom of Solomon. He had a good reading voice, everybody said so. Just like that Graham boy out of North Carolina, he made everything sound like poetry. Not in that sing-song rhyming way that can make the eardrums throb, but in that soothing fashion of a mother's melody.

When Mayor preached, people were inspired. They went away from Sunday service ready to rise up on Monday and get on with the chore of life. He told them stories that stayed with them clean through Saturday and sometimes beyond. He was funny. Still is. How else do you explain a wad of aluminum keeping mosquitoes away?

"I researched it on the internet," he says. "It's a pesticide-free bug repellent."

He might be right. There were no noticeable skeeters that day.

Few people would invite Mayor to church nowadays. One look at him and a person just knows he isn't the churchgoing type, not unless the church has more than a coffee bar inside. He's long past the age where he needs to go looking for pretty girls. He's wise enough now to know nearly every girl is as pretty as the next one, if you study them the right way. And *God* is only a word he uses when he's riled up or trying to be animated.

But Mayor remembers without any hesitation that day he gave his last sermon.

"I was standing up there at that podium. I don't know what

I was saying, but whatever it was, when I looked out over the people, they were crying. Men and women alike. Crying."

Mayor leaned forward, elbows on his knees. He looked up from beneath the shade of thicket brows. "That scared me. Seeing how much power I had over those people."

Cuss words crossed his mind and his lips as he recalled the power of that moment.

"I could see how easy it would be to manipulate a crowd like that," Mayor says.

He walked out the doors of that church and never went back.

★

I've thought a lot about what Mayor told me that summer's day as we sat out on his porch daring skeeters to come hither. Those that don't know him might consider him aimless, but they'd be wrong. Mayor lives a well-intentioned, albeit unconventional, life. He paints portraits on canvases and sometimes murals on the bathroom walls. He reads books and is a bestselling author himself. He still likes women in all shapes and colors.

But there are those who look at his outward appearance and sum him up as a man in need of the saving grace of Jesus. They'd look at the whiskey glass sitting next to his laptop or the vacuum cleaner sitting in tall grass and they'd take pity on him, or worse, judge him as a man lost. But that day, listening to his stories, I realized something: Mayor is a man of integrity. I fought an urge to throw my arms around his neck and kiss him on the cheek. He'll probably be disappointed to hear that. Mayor likes such gratitude.

He could have decided to take advantage of those people weeping there in that church but he didn't. He could have used his skill as a storyteller, his natural charm and boyish good-looks to manipulate others. He could have led those people down roads of gold, and stuffed his pockets full of their shekels while they followed him merrily. Many a crooked evangelist and pastor and bestselling author has done that very thing.

But Mayor had more respect for those good-hearted people, and maybe more respect for the God that created us all, than to use his skills for his own selfish ambition and financial gain.

THE AMBASSADOR

MOONSHINE PRESERVED THE FINGERS HIS BROTHER, NEXT-in-line up from him, chopped from the Ambassador's hand when he was only two years of age. The older boy didn't mean to do his younger brother no harm. It was an accident.

There were three brothers tending the firewood chore. Since he was the youngest, he had the job of gathering the split wood and carrying it in the house to his momma. The toddler reached up at an inopportune moment just as his brother brought down the ax to split a piece of wood in two. He drew back his right hand, minus the middle finger and the one between it and the pinky.

The diced fingers are the cause of him being a southpaw. He'd been reaching for that wood with his right hand but after he lost those fingers, he began to use his left hand for everything.

The Ambassador is 80 now but he still has the fingers his momma rinsed and placed in a jar. She'd tried to cover them with what alcohol was in the house at the time but it wasn't enough. The jar was only about a quarter full. So she grabbed his daddy's white lightening, the whiskey he brewed himself, and topped the fingers off with some of that.

"It was strong stuff," the Ambassador says. "Those fingers

have been in that jar seventy-eight years now and they look just like they did the day they were put in there. They have the fingernails on them and the dirt underneath 'em."

For years the fingers saturated in moonshine in that jar at his Granny's house, but eventually his granny passed them along to the older brother, the one that did the chopping. They weren't kept for superstitious reasons but for matters much more practical than that. They are talking points. A show-and-tell item, like photos from that trip to Greece last year or the jade Buddha brought back from the Far East. The fingers are the remnants of the life the boys had before their parents split up and went their separate ways. Their father to the grasslands of Texas and their young momma to the piney woods in Alabama.

It wasn't until after the Ambassador grew to a full man and married that his brother entrusted him with his own fingers.

"I've been taking care of these, but they are yours now," his brother said, handing over the jar.

Everybody had taken such good care of the toddler's digits that the Ambassador just didn't feel right about getting rid of them.

"I couldn't just throw them away," he says. That's how come he still has them after all these years. Granted they ain't much good to him, pickled, but it's the principal of the thing.

His daughter asked if she could have the family talisman after he died, but he told her, "No, Baby-girl. When my mortal body leaves this earth, my fingers are going with me."

The Ambassador has been preparing for the moment of his passing since he got saved at a revival meeting when he was twelve years old. There's some that might question his salvation at that age, given the way he carried on when he got into the service and all but the Ambassador remembers that moment of salvation with clarity.

"I may have been influenced by this half-aunt of mine that was only three years older than me. She got saved that same night."

He was sitting beside her when she leaned over and said something to him during the altar call.

"I don't know if she said, 'Let's you and I go,' or if she said, 'I'm going.' She said something to me and I automatically got up and went to the front and knelt down at the altar."

Someone, a deacon likely, came and knelt by the young boy and prayed with him. The preacher had laid it all out pretty plainly.

"I didn't have to do nothing to be lost. I was already lost in my status quo. If I accepted Jesus Christ as Lord, I would be saved forever more. That looked to me to be the right way to go," he says.

Young boys and girls don't get much opportunity these days to accept Jesus Christ as their Lord and Savior. Not many preachers give altar calls any more. People lost favor with such invitations. But the Ambassador figures if he hadn't got saved that night, kneeling there at that altar, it's likely he never would have.

From the appearance of things on the outside, not much changed for the Ambassador after he asked Jesus into his heart.

"I did things and said things not pleasing to the Lord, especially when I was in the military," he says.

But all that's getting ahead of the story.

After his daddy split, his momma raised five boys by her lonesome. The kinfolk tried to get her to give up her boys but Big Momma was a stubborn woman who loved her boys fiercely. She wasn't about to give one of them up. Anybody who tried to argue her out of those boys was wasting their breath.

They lived in the backwoods of South Alabama, so far back

they had to pipe in sunshine. Their home was a section house, just off the crossroads, near the train tracks. There was a small grocery, a couple of more section houses, but the nearest church was two miles up yonder. And the nearest town further yet.

They kept a garden out back, in the winter and the summer. So they never went hungry, even in the worst of the Depression.

"Those who didn't have anything to begin with didn't have anything to lose," the Ambassador says. "We didn't have much use for money then."

Big Momma had grown up on a share-cropping farm, she knew how to make do with very little. She was industrious. She picked cotton. She took in washing and ironing. When the boys got big enough, she put them to work.

The Ambassador was ten when he got his first paying job. A farmer had come by the house, wanting to hire one of Big Momma's older boys but they were all hired out that summer. So Big Momma told the man that if he thought her ten-year-old could do the job she'd let the boy go with him. The farmer sized up the little Ambassador and reckoned he could. Then Big Momma asked the boy if he wanted the job. He did.

"I'd get up in the mornings and help the farmer feed the hogs and do other chores," the Ambassador says. "He paid me $3.50 a week."

The farmer and his wife were real nice to the boy. They treated him like he was one of their kids. The boy would go home once a week on Saturday nights. He'd give Big Momma the money he earned. It felt good to help out his momma that a' way.

Only once did he keep back some of the money for his self. It was after he'd finished his last week. The farmer drove him into the nearest town of Opp, Alabama. He had some errands to run, so he urged the boy to take some of his money and go to the movie house.

But the boy didn't want to. He'd never been to a movie house before. All he knew was that they were dark inside and he wasn't keen on the notion of giving other people his money just so he could go sit in the dark. Instead he spent fifteen cents on an ice cream cone and a block of ice that he carried home to his momma in the farmer's rig.

When he was twelve, Big Momma moved the boys to town and she got a job in the textile plant, sewing men's underwear, shirts, and pants. His older brother worked there too, but when the boy got old enough, he dropped out of school and joined the service. His time in Europe not only took him away from Big Momma, it took him away from God as well.

"When I was in the military I lived like the devil," he says. "I had a respect for the things of God, and I had a fear of God. I still believed everything in the Bible is 100 percent true, but I guess you could say I backslid."

Things between him and God didn't get straightened out until he returned from Germany. He was assigned to duty at Fort Benning, Georgia, but he had brothers in nearby Phenix City, Alabama. The Army allowed him to live off base and drive into work.

He told his older brother, "I'll live with you but I don't want no preaching at me."

Agreed, said the older brother. He placed a gospel of John on the bedside stand but he did not harangue his brother about God. On occasion he'd invite him to church, or to a revival meeting. Once the soldier took him up on it, and when the altar call came around, the soldier went forward. Not for salvation, he already had that.

"To become a Christian you have to believe, and as long as you don't disbelieve, you're still saved. You may say things and do things wrong and even some terrible things, but as long as you still believe you're saved. Christ isn't going to die for you over and over again."

So it wasn't salvation he sought, but forgiveness for his willful ways. As he knelt there at that altar that night, he felt the call of the Lord upon his life. He knew he'd go into the ministry, maybe as a preacher or evangelist or missionary.

He was twenty-three when he finished his six-and-a-half years of military service and headed off to Southeastern Bible College. It was while there that the Ambassador encountered some of the crusaders of what would become the Cash-and-Cadillac Gospel.

"There's more of that kind of preaching now than the old line Bible teaching," says the Ambassador.

He was never one to buy into all that nonsense. The Ambassador isn't one to speak ill-will of anyone, especially not a person who professes to shod their feet with the Word of God. But he calls 'em as he sees 'em.

"I don't believe in that name-it-and-claim-it stuff. It's a false doctrine."

And the preachers who preach it?

"They're crooked."

Preachers who go around telling people that God wants them to be rich have their own self-interest at heart. Their churches are storefronts for a gussied-up Ponzi scheme.

"If a preacher is preaching and all his emphasis is on money — if he's saying God needs your help, God needs your money, so send it to me now — back away from that right fast like," the Ambassador warns. "Everything is God's. He don't need mine or your help in having what is already his."

The only thing you can be sure of with a preacher like that is that God won't ever see the money you sacrifice. Go ahead. Imagine a church as a business and the preacher as the CEO. The more money the CEO brings in, the bigger he grows the business, the fatter his paycheck.

Of course, it takes a lot of players to build a Ponzi pyramid. Preachers who tell their congregations that God wants to prosper them might be teaching a false doctrine but they know their audience.

"Smooth taking might be how a fellow gets away with it but it's not just him," the Ambassador says. "It's the people in the congregation. People want to hear the things he's saying. He's telling us things that make us feel good — that we can be prosperous."

All these smooth-talkers remind the Ambassador of a man he worked with years ago, who had made a fortune in the grocery business by selling brooms.

"He said he kept the brooms by the cash register and sold one to every person who went out the door."

Sometimes the customer would protest that the broom wasn't theirs, and so the fellow wouldn't ring it up then, but that was a small percentage of folks. Most just paid for the broom and took it on home. Prosperity preachers are employing the same sales techniques.

"I hate to say this, but since we're talking facts and all, if you went and listened to some of these people you'll find that they preach real good. They might say you're cheating God if you don't give this or that. They say it in such a smooth way that when that offering plate comes around, even a weasel can't let it pass without putting something in it."

Those preachers are selling useless goods to people who don't know any better. They are passing out brooms at the door.

"There's a little bit of larceny in all of us," the Ambassador says. "Everybody wants to make another dollar."

Justifying their exploitation of God comes natural to these folks. The Ambassador recalled a sermon he heard some years back.

"It was a lady preacher but a man could have said the same thing. She said her wardrobe was getting a little low and she needed a new outfit. One day a truck stopped at her daddy's store to drop off some stuff and a box fell out of the back of the man's truck. She went to retrieve the box after the man left and there was a dress in her size, exactly her size.

"She said she was so thankful to have recovered that because it was a box the Lord had dropped off for her."

What a load of dookey, the Ambassador thought.

"I don't believe that no more than I can fly. That man got careless and left the box on the tailgate of his truck. That man came by the store regular. They knew who he was and where he was from. They could have returned the box. They should have returned the box. To say that God threw it out there for her, well I just didn't believe anything that woman said from that point on."

The thing all these glossy preachers have in common is a silver tongue. They mix a little bit of the truth into their sermons and try to pass it off as the gospel truth. And the thing of it is, so few people really know the Bible anymore, it's easy to lead most folks off course. They may think they are getting the Bible, but what they are really getting is a sugar substitute. It'll go down easy enough, but just you wait and see, there's going to be a bitterness to it eventually.

The Ambassador doesn't serve up the gospel on a silver platter. He gives it to people straight up, same as that moonshine his fingers have soaked in all these years. Every trip to the local mall becomes an opportunity for the Ambassador to talk to people about Jesus.

"I find me a spot and sit down and if someone comes along I'll talk to them about the Lord. I don't have any set approach but I don't grab them and say, 'Look, are you saved?' I try to find out what interests them and connect what they are saying to something in the Bible."

A person doesn't need a ticket-only arena or a megascreen showplace to lead others to the Lord. The Ambassador has prayed with near strangers right there in the Ocala mall as Gator fans passed by. He's been a source of encouragement to many.

"A few Christians who have grown cold in the Lord have reconcentrated their lives and started going back to church because of the talks we've had," he said.

Talking about the Lord is how the Ambassador earned his handle. It was his wife's uncle who first encouraged him to take up the Ham radio. Uncle Gene had been a Ham radio enthusiast since before World War II. But the Ambassador didn't take it up until five years ago when he had a little extra time to spare.

He began chatting with another gentleman, a blind fellow from Panama City. They spent a lot of time talking about the Lord and it was from that friendship that the Ambassadors for Christ group formed. They planned out an hour-long show and had seven folks check-in during that first hour. Now they are up to 1300 hams. Most days they hear from about 25 to 30 of those during the show. Each one comes on and reads a scripture or gives a testimony.

But it's the suicidal people who've called that the Ambassador remembers best. There's been a handful of them over the years that have rung him up to offer their thanks. They've recounted their despair, how they thought there was no way out but to take their own lives. But then they heard a word of encouragement or maybe conviction from the Ambassador or one of his cohorts and picked up a Bible, instead of a gun.

"They might still be having a hard time with their problems but now they are able to face them," the Ambassador says.

To hear the Ambassador tell it, Christianity isn't about searching for a way to get your palms greased. It's about looking for the opportunity to be the hands and feet of Christ. Even if that hand is short a couple of fingers.

THE LAWYER

S HE LEFT HIM $2 MILLION BUT IT COST THE LAWYER HIS JOB. By 2006, he'd been with the Fortune 500 company for twenty-two years, working his way up to Deputy General Counsel. He was fifty-four years old, and the father of three bi-racial boys he'd adopted and one biological son, who had died ten years earlier from a self-inflicted gunshot wound.

The Lawyer met Miss Nell after The Boss sent him to Austin, Texas, to straighten out some mess between her and a renegade salesman looking to swindle Miss Nell out of her territory.

The salesman had underestimated the mean old Dutch woman. That's the title Miss Nell ascribed to herself. She could be a worthy adversary if you crossed her, as the salesman had done.

Miss Nell was threatening to sue the Fortune 500 company.

I want you on a plane to Austin, tomorrow. And I want this thing fixed right away. Those had been the marching orders The Boss had given The Lawyer.

Miss Nell was waiting for him when he arrived. The seventy-five-year-old wore an off-the-rack dress, sensible shoes, and her trademark bright red lipstick. Her eyes were bright and energetic. Her mind even more so.

She didn't have a college degree, but she'd grown up in the Valley with LBJ and Lady Bird. She worked for him when he was Congressman Johnson. She'd also worked for Senator Lloyd Bentsen and some other fellow who was a close friend of Senator Ted Kennedy's.

Miss Nell had been married once. She married Dewitt just weeks before he shipped out for Europe in 1942. While he marched across Africa, Italy, France, and Germany, she made do in Texas. After the war ended and he returned home safely, the two never had any children of their own. So when Dewitt died in 1968, Miss Nell, an only child herself, was all alone again. That's when she went to work.

They say she knew everybody in East Texas and more than plenty in the state's biggest cities. All those contacts paid off when she became a saleswoman for the Fortune 500 company. By the time the Lawyer met her, she was living comfortably off the commissions she made from the accounts she'd sold. Not in the lap of luxury, mind you. The Lawyer reckons that she never made more than $35,000 in any given year.

It didn't take the Lawyer but a couple of hours to straighten things out between the cantankerous Dutch woman and the upstart salesman trying to hone in on her accounts, and less than that to charm Miss Nell altogether.

"I think she was expecting some high-pressure, cigar-smoking lawyer," he says. "But I knew how to be gentle and diplomatic."

It was one of the many life-skills he'd learned from his preacher father.

★

His daddy was a gentle man, who knew how to turn away an

angry person with a soft word. He was well-loved by every church he pastored. There were only four of them in a lifetime of service.

The few times he was called by a new church, he would not allow the search committee to tell him in advance what the financial considerations would be. He'd stop them on the spot before they divulged any numbers.

"I'm not worried about any specifics," he said. "I'll pray about this."

To his family he said, "If God wants me there he'll provide for us."

He had integrity, this preacher man did. He knew his own heart, knew that it would act out of selfish gain, given a chance. He never gave it that chance.

The boy paid attention to the way his father lived.

"When I think of my childhood I think of Opie on The Andy Griffith Show," the Lawyer says. "I could identify with him."

He grew up in a small southern town where the doctor never charged the family a dime, although the doctor was a Presbyterian and the Preacher was a Baptist. The druggist would offer the kids ice cream cones whenever they came by his store. It seemed everybody in town was always watching out for the preacher's kids.

That sort of treatment always made the Lawyer feel special, but his preacher daddy never taught his son to go around expecting others to grant him favor. He was taught sacrifice, not entitlement.

"Even as young kids we were made aware that we were a family that was in ministry together," the Lawyer says. "We had to be careful about our money."

A luxury item was the six-pack of coke his momma bought every week for the family of four.

"A couple of times a week I'd split one of those with my sister."

He was expected to be a good steward of all the many blessings God had given him, but blessings were rarely equated with consumer goods.

"My parents never said that I should expect God's favor. They taught that we would not have extra but that we were expected to be good stewards of what we did have."

He remembers a sermon his father taught about a rich man.

"Dad talked about how some Christians have this view that if they followed Christ everything would fall their way. He gave an illustration of a very wealthy man trying to close another deal while on his death bed. One of his close aides came to him saying, 'You have millions and millions, how much is enough for you?' And the rich man replied, 'Only a little more.'"

His father would use that story to talk about the heart of man and how greedy man could be.

"No matter what he has, he always wants a little more," Preacher said.

Jesus did not promise us material wealth, the Lawyer says. He promised a life of sacrifice. That was the lesson his father taught the Lawyer.

But as a boy he heard a different message from the television preacher.

"The earliest I heard about prosperity preaching, the name-it-claim-it stuff, was from Rev. Ike. He was this really entrancing and entertaining TV evangelist who was unashamedly materialistic.

"He would sell these prayer cloths and he would ask, 'Do

you want one or two Cadillacs in your garage? I will send you a prayer shawl and if you pray over it, you will have money.' He would read testimonials from people who'd already bought the prayer cloths and they'd gotten some unexpected check in the mail."

The Rev. Ike also sold coins with his likeness on one side.

"On the one side, under Rev. Ike's face, it read, 'Good Luck'. He would flip the coin over and it said 'Blessings and Prosperity,'" the Lawyer says. "He'd flip that coin and say, 'Look, it's good luck.' Then he'd flip it again, 'Look, it's on blessings and prosperity. You can't lose with the stuff I use.'"

That was Rev. Ike's catch-all phrase — You can't lose with the stuff I use. And the message was clear, even to a ten-year-old boy: "If you do what I tell you to do, you'll get rich, or at least a lot richer than you are right now."

When the son asked his preacher dad about the Reverend Ike, his dad replied, "That's not what the Bible says, boy. The Bible says we'll have trouble in this world but fear not because I have overcome this world. The Reverend Ike is taking advantage of people."

The boy grew into a man and into the Lawyer but he never forgot the lessons his preacher dad taught him. He didn't forget Reverend Ike either. At the Fortune 500 company where the Lawyer worked he noticed that many of the salespeople acted like the Reverend.

"It's remarkable the number of people in sales who professed a faith in Jesus Christ and the number of the sales managers who almost exclusively hired Christians."

The Lawyer had to handle the complaints of discrimination that came in from the sales staff that weren't Christians. Those employees that made no claims to having the favor of

God upon their lives the way their Jesus-branded peers did. But even without the Jesus logo, the Lawyer noticed they shared a similar-minded philosophy. "A lot of people in sales mirrored the teaching that if you work hard enough and stay positive enough, prosperity will come your way."

Is this a result of Corporate America co-opting the Prosperity Gospel? Or is the Prosperity Gospel the by-product of Corporate America? In or out of the church, people who embrace this worldview are primarily concerned with what's in it for them.

The Lawyer noticed one more thing about the people in the Fortune 500 company. The higher up the corporate ladder they climbed, the less they needed Jesus or heeded his teachings. They might attend a church, but it was usually one of the churches where other wealthy people were present. It was just one more venue for networking — a way to grow the business on their days off.

"There are exceptions, but on the management side I didn't see a lot of strong interest in mainstream Christianity," he says.

He paid attention to all that he saw and he formed his own theory about the seductive power of money.

"The things we chase after in life, it's all a mist."

Like Solomon said.

"At first we worry about survival — what am I going to eat, where am I going to find shelter?" the Lawyer explains. "If we get past survival then we begin to think about storing up, like squirrels in winter. There's really no thought at this point of, I'm storing up so all the other squirrels will think I'm great. That comes later.

"Right now, we're just trying to build a cushion. Once we get the cushion built, we begin to realize, I have some riches here. How can I make my pile bigger? Once our pile gets big enough, power becomes the thing we have to have. We have to build our power so we can become king and we don't care who we have to step on to get there. In fact, that's part of the fun — stepping on others. From then on out it's protecting our castle and crushing any rebellions."

The Lawyer saw these struggles over and over again during his days with the Fortune 500 company. He even participated in a few of these scuffles for power, himself. But he noticed that every man or woman who got to the top of the heap felt a sense of disappointment once they were there.

"They end up asking themselves, 'Gee, is this all there is?'"

Yes. For those who live their lives seeking after consumer goods, that's all there is. For others, like the Lawyer, life goes far beyond the financial gain of the here and now.

"Christ never, ever equated abundant life with financial security or financial wealth," he says.

The Lawyer remembers that whenever his father performed the funerals for the wealthy people in the church, invariably someone would inquire, "Preacher, tell me, how much did he leave behind?"

"Daddy would reply, 'All of it.'"

★

Miss Nell started calling the Lawyer every couple of weeks. The phone calls weren't long — maybe twenty minutes. She often retold him the same stories. When he went through a heart-wrenching divorce, she sent him handwritten notes of encouragement. Once a year she would send him twenty-five boxes of Lamme's Chewy Pralines. One was his to keep, the others were for him to deliver to others in the Company's main office. The

Lawyer remembers that they were tasty caramels that could rip out a fellow's fillings if he wasn't careful.

During one of Miss Nell's regular phone calls, she told the Lawyer she didn't have a will, yet. Could he help her? He did, but not by writing up the will himself, but by putting her in touch with another attorney, one who specialized in that sort of thing.

He didn't think much of it when she told him that she was leaving him 10 percent of her estate.

"She played her cards close to the vest. I didn't know how much she had but I didn't think it was very much," he said.

At that time it wasn't. She had a little nest egg that she had culled from a hobby of hers. Miss Nell liked to enter sweepstakes. She would tear the forms out of newspapers and magazines, off the backs of cereal boxes and razors blades. This was in the pre-computer days. An energetic and too often lonely woman like Miss Nell had a lot of time on her hands. She filled it with self-addressed stamped envelopes.

And in 1986 she won $30,000.

She called somebody at the home office of the Company and asked them how she should invest it. Not surprisingly they told her to buy stock in their company and never, ever spend the dividends. So that's what she did. It grew slowly at first, but steadily. By 1996, she had $600,000 in her account.

That was a terrible year for the Lawyer.

His only child, a fourteen-year-old boy from his previous marriage, took his own life.

A person can think of a million reasons why but not a one of them makes any sense. All anyone knows for sure is that the youth was a happy boy who knew he was well-loved in circles near and far.

The loss was and remains indescribable.

The Lawyer doesn't know for sure if it's true, but it's rumored that when Miss Nell learned of the boy's death, she had to be hospitalized. She'd only met the boy once, but she knew how much his father and mother loved him. She knew how much she would have loved a child of her own, had she been fortunate enough to bear any, but she wasn't. Miss Nell had suffered through nine miscarriages. The death of nine children. She understood grief.

She could not give the Lawyer back his son, but she did change her will that year. Instead of 10 percent, he would get half of her estate.

When she told him, he went straight to his boss and told him. He'd done the same thing when she'd first told him that he would get 10 percent.

The Company had no rules, no policy preventing one co-worker from bequeathing something to another. But he didn't want any cause for trouble. No conflicts-of-interests. So he told his superiors and he reminded them year after year after year that Miss Nell had left him 50 percent of her estate, which was continuing to grow, right along with the Company.

He married again and adopted a brown-skinned boy.

Miss Nell was a proud yellow-dog Democrat from the old school. She could be crass in her ways. The Lawyer figured once she learned his son was bi-racial she might decide to change her will again — cutting him entirely out of the will.

But instead she changed. Cleaned up her act. Quit using those nasty racial slurs she'd used all her life.

The moment of her redemption came when she held the adopted son for the first time. He was six months old. She hadn't hardly gotten out of the cab that was carrying her to visit the family when she told the Lawyer, "Hand over that baby."

So he did.

And she puckered up those bright red lips and leaned over to kiss the child and the child, perhaps thinking those lips were candy of some sort, gave her the wettest kiss of her lifetime.

She fell in love with the bi-racial boy on the spot.

It was Miss Nell who kept encouraging the Lawyer to adopt more. In 2003, when Miss Nell was ninety and the Lawyer was 50, he and his wife adopted two more sons, bi-racial twins. One was light. The other was dark.

"Daddy, how come one of my brothers is brown like me and the other brother is white like you?" the eldest son asked.

"That's the way God made us, buddy," he answered.

The Lawyer fretted about the age gap. He'd be in his late sixties before any of the boys graduated from high school, but thanks to Miss Nell, he didn't worry about putting them through college. He knew the gift she was leaving would provide for that.

After Miss Nell died, he saw her gift as God's providential provision.

"I didn't summon this money to myself. I've tried that before and it never has taken," the Lawyer says, laughing.

"I always looked at what Nell was leaving me as a providential thing. But I, in no way, ever said to God, 'If I adopt these children I know you will send me wealth untold.' I never made a deal with God. I never named-it-and-claimed-it. I never thought if I do this good thing, then wealth will come my way. The expected inheritance from Nell did not impact whether I was going to adopt or not. But it was comforting to know there was something there to help me with the boys."

He would need it more than he knew. Once the Company learned the size of Miss Nell's gift — her paltry investment of $30,000 had grown to $5 million and the Lawyer stood to inherit half of that — they changed their policy and dismissed the Lawyer, two years prior to retirement age. They had never made an issue of the money when they thought Miss Nell didn't have much. What did they care if the Lawyer got a measly $15,000 from some forlorn old soul?

But the matter turned ugly when word got out that Miss Nell's gift totaled in the millions. Somebody in-house set out to get the Lawyer, or more specifically, to get his job. They tried to swipe it from him just like that renegade salesman who had tried to take over Miss Nell's territory. The Lawyer threatened to sue. The Company backed down. They didn't give him his job back but they did cut a deal so that he could retain his retirement. The Laywer was glad Miss Nell wasn't around to see all that. It would have broken her heart. She'd been such a stalwart supporter of the Company for so long.

As had he.

But companies, even Fortune 500 companies, are made from mist. Sometimes, it grows so thick you can't see anything else, but then, lickety-quick, everything you work for can all be gone with the snap of a finger or the bullet from a gun.

The Lawyer has never forgotten the lesson the death of his first-born son taught him — the distinction between what really matters in life and what is of no account.

"We think this is the only life that matters but it's not. This is a dress rehearsal for the eternal life to come. Are you living in the temporal or in the eternal?" he asks.

THE VETERAN

BUTTERBEAN SITS AT THE VETERAN'S BEDSIDE. SHE'S A JUNK-yard dog. The Veteran pulled her from underneath a trailer parked up at Ault's Auto Parts and, in so doing, earned Butterbean's companionship, something she so seldom grants, seeing how she truly is a junkyard dog down to her very core.

Butterbean wears a perpetual scowl upon her brow. She's worried about him, and rightly so. The Veteran wears a hospital gown, even at home. That ring he designed, the one with the Manchu Golden Dragon crafted from diamonds, is in the safe in his office. He worked with a big city jeweler on the design for that ring. He'd sketched it out just as he wanted it. He was so proud of that fancy ring and all it represented.

It bears his name, engraved in gold, and a tiny replica Purple Heart on one side and a flash of lightning, the insignia for the 25th Infantry Division on the other. It has that horrible date — May 28, 1970 — raised in relief so that a fellow can rub a thumb and forefinger across it and recall those events even while carrying on a conversation with somebody about something totally unrelated, like how the garden is doing this year or the gains in the stock market, not that there have been many of those lately.

But the Veteran can't talk much these days. If he's worried about the stock market and the hits he's taken there he never says. Mostly he lies in the hospital bed, the one with the gel mattress that keeps him from getting bed sores, in the sun room of his Tennessee home staring up at the ceiling fan. Or maybe, hopefully, he sees the lights and spirals of heaven. The gate isn't that far off now, just a few days or less up the road.

He doesn't ask to be fed, though he'll eat plenty enough when the Little Woman, who is his wife of thirty-five years, stands by his bed and spoons up bites of potatoes and apple-sauce for him. The hands on the clock move slowly as she leans over him, offers a pain pill, and says, "You swallow that now."

"No," he says firmly, but he swallows anyway.

The Veteran was never one to take instructions from others. He still doesn't like to be bossed around.

"I'm going to take your teeth and clean them," she says, pulling out his lower choppers first.

The Veteran is sixty years of age, but he's had false teeth since he was twenty. He lost the ones God gave him in that gun battle near the Cambodian border when a sniper blew off his lower jaw and killed Doc, the medic who yanked him to safety and died doing it.

Doc had a young wife back home. She was pregnant with the couple's baby daughter. She raised that girl with help from her family and Doc's. She's never remarried.

The Veteran left the battlefield that day and never returned, except in that place of his mind where it seems he can never get away from it all. He spent the next nineteen months at Walter Reed relearning things a toddler knows how to do: how to talk, how to swallow, how to chew, how to drink from a cup, and how not to dribble while doing any of the aforementioned tasks.

If he could will death, the Veteran would have died that day in the battlefield, alongside the medic. If he trusted you, and he had the ability, which he doesn't now, he'd tell you that he spent too much of his life wishing it all away.

Survivors' guilt, the experts call it. Post-Traumatic Stress Disorder. PTSD for short.

The Veteran didn't have any idea what to call it. For years, he couldn't talk about the darkness that made him such an ornery person to live with. Lucky for him he married a patient woman, one that loved him in spite of himself. He never told her but he'd sometimes tell others that the Little Woman was a godsend. Without her by his side, he'd been dead a long time ago.

He should have told her.

She needed to hear those words.

She's taken time off from her job to tend to him. Her days are spent at his side, spoon-feeding him, cleaning his teeth, turning him, bathing him, covering and uncovering him, and trimming the beard he grew as a young man to cover the hideous scars that sniper inflicted.

He doesn't need a ring to remember that day. He's remembered it every single morning for decades now. Every time he looked in the mirror and put in his teeth.

Sometimes he asks her, "Where's my stuff?"

She knows exactly what he's talking about. It's that way with people who've been partners for near about a lifetime. She goes to the safe in his office and turns the black-and-white dial, listening for the click of the code. Then she gathers his stuff to carry back to the sunroom for him.

★

His stuff consists of his billfold and that ring that he designed before that trip to the Vietnam Memorial Wall in D.C. where he met up with Doc's grown daughter and her momma.

The three of them read Doc's name together at a Veterans Day ceremony. They stood there in the dark, shivering from the cold and the grief, and read from a long list of names. It takes four days of reading twenty-four hours around the clock to get through the complete list of over 58,000 names of men and women killed- or missing-in-action. The Veteran wore his leather coat and his cap with the red and yellow colors across it. Colors from the South Vietnamese flag, colors meant to represent a freedom that existed in ideology only.

Ideals are the things that Congress and knuckleheads claim to draft war over. Mostly, though they won't hardly admit it, it's for money's sake. Some will even volunteer to do the fighting that Congress bids them to do. During the Veteran's era, men went to war because they were ordered to go, they didn't have a choice. They fought that war mostly for the sake of getting their buddies out alive.

Failing to do that, they never forgive themselves. The Veteran once penned a poem that hangs in the hallway of his brick home. It reads in part:

God knows I wonder why?
I was chosen to survive.
My choice was to die.
My guilt remains.

It's a fine home. Not the biggest one in town by any stretch, but it's comfortable and built so tight a mouse would have to knock at the door to gain entrance. They raised their two kids in the home where he now lays dying.

The Veteran taught the girl how to shoot hoops in the driveway and the boy to shoot trap in the woods out back. It was a skill that came in handy years later when the boy shipped out to fight that War on Terror. Unlike his father, the boy came home unscathed.

There's a get-well card on the glass-topped, bronzed-bear coffee table that the Veteran bought on an impulse. It cost him a wad. He surprised himself with the purchase because the Veteran cultivated a reputation for being pretty scotch. He didn't live in the pursuit of money, necessarily, but he wasn't one to waste it either. But by the time he bought that table the cancer was back and he was beginning to understand the value of money, and of life.

"All these years I spent wishing I was dead and now here I am fighting to save my life," he said in that year that turnip-shaped tumor was discovered inside his head.

The card is from the Ruth Sunday School Class at the Baptist church he and the Little Woman have attended all these years. "Prayers can bring about miracles that is why we never stop praying for you," the card reads.

For far too many years the Veteran spent more time in the bars than he did in church. But then he had that accident, the one that really did almost kill him. He came to face-down in a ditch. The next week he went to church with his wife and reconcentrated his life to Christ.

He became a student of the Bible, taught Sunday school classes and went to church real regular. Faith in God can heal a person from the inside out, but there are some scars, like the ones on the Veteran's face, that remain.

He spent the springtime planting a garden big enough to feed half the county, and every summer picking and delivering pole beans and tomatoes, corn and potatoes. In the autumn, he'd hunt rabbits with the beagles.

Not long ago, he gave his beagles away.

It's winter now, and he lays dying.

★

He asked for his stuff the other day. The Little Woman went to the safe and retrieved the man's earthly treasures.

He slept with his billfold clutched to his chest all night long.

The next morning his wife found his precious ring. It had slipped from his fingers and was pressed up against his thigh. If you could see his thighs now it would make you flinch. Those once muscular legs that bore the weight of one of the nation's most decorated soldiers are inflamed and ulcerated, the result of the cancer spreading.

And so it goes.

When he draws his last breath he will leave it all behind. The diamond ring and the golden medals. The fine home and the garden neglected. The leather billfold and the Rolex watch.

The Veteran was sitting in the lobby of a swanky D.C. hotel with friends once when a man came along and inquired of him, "How much did you give for that watch?"

"I give what I paid for it," he answered, laughing.

Do not be deceived. Truly, it's not what we amass in this short time known as life that matters, but how we spend what time we are granted. The Veteran didn't always spend his wisely. Few of us ever do.

When he passes, you can be sure the Little Woman will be there at his side, clutching his hand and weeping for the man she loved more than life itself, the way Jesus has loved each of us.

THE BEAUTICIAN

TWO WHITE LEATHER SOFAS STEP BACK FROM ONE ANOTHER, as if they are in a silent standoff over the tangerine-colored rug between them. Their chrome feet planted on gleaming hardwood. A petite woman with finely-sculpted calves and arms holds a blow dryer in one hand as she pulls a round brush with the other through a client's brunette hair. The Beautician works her way around the flamingo-necked woman, blowing and pulling, as if she's waiting for some unheard tune to stop playing so she, too, can finally sit down.

She wears a pair of nude-colored patent leather flats. She splurged on the designer shoes during a trade show trip to New York City. They cost $500 on sale. That's a steal-of-a-deal in the neighborhood where the Beautician lives and works.

There are people in town who buy shoes at Payless, but those people don't frequent the Beautician's shop. They get their kitchen-sink hair dye from a box at Walmart. The Beautician has earned the reputation as being the best colorist in these parts. She does not cut hair. For that service, you'll need to go elsewhere. Her fees rival that of an hour-long consultation with a reputable neurosurgeon.

If she had only a fraction of the wealth of her clients, she'd do so many really good things with it. She tells God that every chance she gets, reciting the litany of goodwill she could do, if only he'd see fit to bless her.

She'd start by helping the children in Zimbabwe. It's a pitiful shame when children die from something as preventable as cholera. She'd give some money to help rebuild homes destroyed by Katrina. She used to make regular trips to New Orleans, where she'd poke around the Quarter and meet friends for supper.

If she had the money of God, she'd build a bigger home, one with an entertainment room, so she could host the church youth group or have the singles in for supper once a month. Maybe put in a carriage house out back, for the missionaries who come to town and for visiting pastors.

★

The Jesus Hawker is on the telly again, making empty promises.

"Tonight is the poorest you'll ever be again," he says.

All you have to do is send in your seed money.

"If you can't trust God for $58 you'll never be debt-free," he says. Act now. In Jesus' name!

"Tomorrow, somebody's gonna drive a Mercedes."

It could be you. If only you'll have enough faith.

What is it you seek? A bigger home, a luxurious new car, a promotion and a fat paycheck, a trip to the Holy Land, or perhaps a plasma TV? You've got to give your way into the future.

"If you've ever decided to obey the Holy Spirit, go to the phone right now."

Make that call. Plant that seed.

"My goal is for three hundred people to hear the wisdom

that God gives my heart for them to become millionaires for the sake of the kingdom of God," Mike Murdock continues.

Murdock is just one of the many pitchmen featured on the Inspiration Network. Headquartered in Charlotte, North Carolina, the Inspiration Network rose up from the heap that once was Jim and Tammy Faye Baker's PTL empire. And just like its gilded predecessor, the Inspiration Network is pulling in millions in donations, a reported $70 million in 2007.

Inspiration Network boasts a diverse audience of devotees, thanks, in part, to the variety of religious leaders featured on the network, some of whom do not embrace or endorse a prosperity gospel and many of whom are at least trying to make an impact for Christ. The list of those featured on the network is long, but it includes the very staid Rev. Charles Stanley out of Atlanta, the boisterous Bishop T.D. Jakes, the spirited Joyce Meyer, and the always genial Rev. James Robison.

David Cerullo is CEO and chief Jesus-hawker at Inspiration Network. Nepotism earned him that role. It was his father, Morris Cerullo, who bought out the Bakker's fallen empire in 1990. The network's owners and name may have changed but the message has not. Why should it?

It's a tried-and-true equation. Promise folks that God will make them richer than they are today if only they'll invest in the kingdom of God right here and right now, and you can be sure that somebody in that twenty-four-hour audience of 54 million cable and satellite TV households is going to write a check. Probably a whole lot of somebodies.

Heck, if only half of them send in a buck, you've still made enough money to build yourself a sweet place up on Lake Keowee, South Carolina, the way David Cerullo is doing.

It's not like David and his wife, Barbara, needed a bigger

place. They've been living in a 12,000-square-foot home worth $1.7 million in Charlotte, North Carolina. David draws a salary of $1.5 million, making him one of the best paid CEOs of the religious organizations tracked by watchdog groups. His wife and children are reportedly on the payroll for the company as well.

The lake house, currently under construction in western South Carolina, will reportedly cost $4 million and will also be approximately 12,000 square feet, including 2,000 square feet for a screened-in porch.[1] The house sits on a lot that cost nearly another million.

Cerullo's critics note that he has continued this gluttonous lifestyle even while employees at Inspiration Network have faced job cuts, wage freezes, and a halt to matching funds for 401(k) accounts.[2]

South Carolina taxpayers are even helping to fund the construction of the network's new headquarters in Indian Land, South Carolina. The state gave the network a $1.2 million economic development grant to help pay for roads, water, and sewers, all part of a $26 million incentive package.[3]

That Cerullo and his ilk are able to swindle good-hearted people in the name of Jesus as South Carolina's unemployment rate has soared to 12.1 percent and the nation's continues to climb is nothing short of downright criminal.

Or it should be.

But it seems that even in the throes of a recession or depression, there are a couple of growth markets that remain impervious to the economic downturn — the lottery and prosperity evangelism.

"In tough economic times, you'll find that there are a couple of growth industries. One is the lottery and the other is prosperity preachers," said Warren Smith. Smith works with Wall

Watchers, a watchdog group that has become the consumer report for Christian ministries. Wall Watchers website, ministry-watch.com, provides up-to-date information about the financial standings of 500 of the nation's leading ministries. It also assigns a rank based primarily on financial frankness.

The goal is to hold these ministries and their CEOs accountable. Wall Watchers acts, in essence, like the Securities and Exchange Commission. Only, unlike the Securities and Exchange Commission, the folks at Wall Watchers really do provide oversight and take steps to alert consumers when their money may be at risk.

Most of the nation's many ministries do a good job, says Wall Watchers. They point to well-run groups like Compassion International and Wycliffe Bible Translators, and even the Billy Graham Evangelistic Association as examples of ministries that provide financial transparency and accountability. From the get-go Billy Graham established the groundwork of integrity.

"Long before it was ever suggested, my father told his board, 'I want to be audited by an outside auditing firm. I want to make that audit public and we'll let the world know how we've used the money,'" said Franklin Graham.[4]

Contrast that approach with that of Benny Hinn Ministries, which pulls in an estimated hundred million a year. Benny Hinn is the pastor, the president, and the chairman of the board for life. He appoints the vice president and he handpicks his board. His salary is estimated to be between half-a-million to a million dollars a year. He has a ten-million-dollar seaside mansion and the list of perks enjoyed by Hinn and his family rival that of any hedonistic Wall Street CEO.

There is nothing illegal about hawking Jesus, but the watchdog group urges believers to beware. Wall Watchers 2008 tally of ministries who failed to provide financial transparency includes numerous high-profile preachers: Kenneth Copeland, Randy and Paula White, Kenneth Hagin, Paul and Jan Crouch, Tony Alamo, Creflo Dollar, and Bishop Eddie Long. In other words, these are the blackjack dealers in the Praying-for-Dollars lotto.

In 2000, my friend Weezie was in Miramar, on the last leg of a three-week artist tour, when she fell violently ill. Weezie doesn't know whether she fell ill from the fish she ate at dinner or from the mosquitoes biting at her ankles during a lawn party near cholera-infested waters.

She and a roommate had to be escorted back to their room, they were that sick. At one point, Weezie remembers looking over and seeing her roommate's eyes roll back in her head and her tongue thrash forward. Weezie called out her name but the gal never responded.

"I thought she had died, " Weezie says.

Wrestling with a fever and uncontrollable vomiting, Weezie figured she wasn't long for this world herself. Desperate not to be alone in that moment, she reached for the TV remote. There on the screen was a man, speaking her native language: "Do not be afraid," he said. "Jesus is with you."

It was Creflo Dollar.

In her frightened state, Dollar's words were like a cool rag from the hand of heaven. Weezie burst into tears.

"I wept because I knew I was going to be okay," she says.

Three minutes after she hit the remote, Creflo Dollar was replaced by the usual programming, a station that didn't include any native English-speakers. Weezie remains convinced that God used Creflo Dollar to deliver a message to her that day.

The following morning her roommate, who, thankfully, had not died, was wheeled out of the room. Weezie was able to walk out. As soon as she got back to Alabama, Weezie sent a $100 check off to Creflo Dollar.

Though she no longer supports them financially, Weezie does still tune in on occasion.

"There have been times when I've been so depressed and I'll see the pink-haired lady (Jan Crouch), and I think, 'Omygosh, look at that clown.' But if I listen to the words the pink-haired lady is saying, it speaks to my heart."

Yes, these folks beg for money.

Yes, they often exploit people.

Even so, Weezie says, you can't discount the message.

She believes it saved her life.

"I don't prescribe to Creflo Dollar's way of speaking," Weezie says, "but at that particular moment, God sent me that message. It was the only thing on TV that I could understand. Do you know what a remote place I was in, and there was Creflo Dollar? For me it was a revelation."

After Weezie found Jesus in Miramar, Creflo Dollar and some of his ilk have come under more than the scrutiny of an online consumer advocacy group, some are under Senate investigation. They are also under the suspicious scowl of their peers.

★

Americans, who strive for a separation between God and state, paradoxically insist on tattooing God on every minted cent.

In a capitalistic society, where the American dream is equated with having earned the favor of God, the poor can be a hard sell. Those who have plenty cannot escape the deeply-rooted belief that people who live in poverty do so because of their own failures.

The thing that compels millions of hopefuls to take out the

ballpoint pen and send in $58 of seed money to Murdock on the promise that God will repay them tenfold is the very same thing that compelled thousands to place their trust in Wall Street investor Bernie Madoff.

That thing is greed.

Prior to the stock market's nagging arrhythmia and Bernie Madoff, the word *greed* had practically disappeared from the national Lexicon. Trust the people, former President Ronald Reagan decreed as he sought to relax government's regulatory oversight. A free market society works best without those pesky buttinski feds.

"We who live in free market societies believe that growth, prosperity and ultimately human fulfillment are created from the bottom up, not from the top down," Reagan said.

"Only when the human spirit is allowed to invent and create, only when individuals are given a personal stake in deciding economic policies and benefitting from their success — only then can societies remain economically alive, dynamic, progressive and free. Trust the people," Reagan urged. "This is the one irrefutable lesson of the entire postwar period contradicting the notion that rigid government controls are essential to economic development."

Trust the people. They should be allowed to pursue their own self-interests. It was a noble theory, except for one flawed construct — the heart of man. Beyond God's regulatory power, it is selfish, greedy, and deceitful.

Jeremiah 17:9 — "The heart is deceitfully wicked. Who can know it?"

John Wesley surmised: "There is nothing so false and deceitful as the heart of man; deceitful in its apprehensions of things, in the hopes and promises which it nourishes, in the assurances that it gives us; unsearchable by others, deceitful with reference to ourselves, and abominably wicked, so that neither can a man know his own heart, nor can any other know that of his neighbor's."

★

Greed is taught in our homes, our schools, and our churches. It's a national virtue touted in glossy magazines, taught in high school marketing classes, lauded from Fortune 500 platforms and from behind glass-and-chrome pulpits. It's regaled in our theatres and our boardrooms. Be ambitious. Climb to the top. Break the glass ceiling. The feasting table is ready, buddy, come have your fill.

Oh, sure, there have been some who embraced the ascetic values of another era. A few for whom greed remained a virulent sin. Mother Teresa for one, but hey, she was a nun. Nuns aren't tempted by Calvin Klein's underwear, or Paris Hilton's booty.

Rich Mullins was another. Mullins was an award-winning musician and songwriter who could have lived the lavish lifestyle flaunted by the blinged-out cowboys and cowgirls who ride out of Nashville and New York. He purposely avoided the trinkets of fame, and he rejected altogether the Gospel of Entitlement as outright heresy.

Mullins, like Wesley, knew the heart of man. He knew what politicians and preachers denied — he could not trust his own heart. So while other evangelicals schemed to build their empires, praying the prayer of Jabez to increase their platforms and their portfolios, Mullins made his home in a single-wide in one of our nation's poorest regions.

He wisely constructed a defense against the fungus of greed taking root by signing over his income to his church home. No, it was not a farthing, not even a tenth of his royalties, but all of it. A board of elders managed Mullin's money. From his own earnings, they paid him a salary — the average yearly wage for an American worker, and Mullins lived off that. The remaining funds were doled out to charities. Mullins feared that had he been in charge of the money, had he any idea the bounty that his music was producing, he would be too greedy to give it away.

Instead of building a mansion of marble in Brentwood, Mullins moved to the Navajo Nation. He made his bed there among the scrub brush and prickly cacti because Mullins believed, truly believed that it was under the watchful eye of Window Rock that he was able to get a vision for what Christianity ought to look like.

During one of his last concerts, prior to the tragic vehicle accident in 1997 that took his life, Mullins gave an account of his faith: "Jesus said whatever you do to the least of these my brothers you've done it to me. And this is what I've come to think. That if I want to identify fully with Jesus Christ, who I claim to be my savior and Lord, the best way that I can do that is to identify with the poor. This I know will go against the teachings of all the popular evangelical preachers. But they're just wrong. They're not bad, they're just wrong."

They are not bad — they are just wrong, Mullins said.

But, as it turns out, more than a handful are both bad and wrong. Because while Wall Street came crashing down, a slew of evangelicals went rushing to the boom mic and the boob tube to milk this baby for all its worth.

★

Smart, educated, cosmopolitan, intelligent, well-heeled, wealthy people trusted Bernie Madoff. Policy-makers and filmmakers.

Writers and directors. Admin.   nd adjuncts. Editors and
agents. These are the same pati.   people who gathered
at glitzy cocktail parties on New Yo.   er West Side and
derided those living in the double-wide.   .berton, North
Carolina, or in clapboard homes in Mag.   .labama, for
sending in their $58 of seed faith to the gang at .   .iration Net-
work. How is it, they wondered, that these poor souls fail to see
that they are being taken advantage of by these smarmy-looking
preachers?

Yet, this very same group of the nation's high and mighty
and even a group of the average and trusting didn't think twice
about turning over millions and millions of dollars to the elu-
sive Madoff. They were more than willing to give the seventy-
year-old their holdings because rumor had it that Madoff was a
Midas man. Everything that man touched turned to gold. Even
the Securities and Exchange Commission trusted the promi-
nent Wall Street trader. And why shouldn't they? It never occurred to any of them that the former chairman of the Nasdaq
Stock Market might really be a two-bit thug at heart.

By the time it was discovered, Madoff had pilfered an estimated $50 billion from the nation's big and rich. Bernie Madoff
made Entitlement evangelists like David Cerullo and Creflo
Dollar look like two-bit carnie players.

So how is it that the commanders of some of the nation's
leading universities and foundations fell for what Madoff himself referred to as "basically a giant Ponzi scheme"?

By virtue of the very thing that compels others to pick up
a copy of the latest book promising the big rich life now. The
Greek word for it is *pleonexia*. Insatiable desire. Unbridled lust.
A relentless hungering for more of what one already possesses.

Plain, old-fashioned, sinful greed.

★

When my neighbor Ethan MacDonald and his wife, Sara, got married they had several nieces and nephews serve as attendants. Because the children were very young their mothers bribed the kids with the promise of candy. Following each successful, rehearsed stroll down the aisle the children were rewarded with brightly colored chewies.

On the day of the wedding, when one of the youngest nephews reached the church altar, he hollered out, "WHERE'S MY CANDY?"

Many of us treat God like that. We stomp our feet and make demands at the altar of the Almighty. Like the Beautician, we believe that if we uphold our half of the bargain by putting our trust in God, then he ought to do better by us. Give us the stone mansion with the carriage house out back where we can host the missionaries come to town and the visiting pastors. God ought to bulk up our portfolios so we can better afford to give $50 a month to the kids in Zimbabwe.

We make a habit of standing before God, yelling, "WHERE IS MY REWARD?"

We don't yet understand that being in God's presence is the reward.

THE MOGUL

H E WAS A RICH MAN. A VERY, VERY, VERY WEALTHY MAN. The Mogul was only twenty-seven years old in 1961 when his father died, leaving him to assume the helm of the modest auto dealership that the elder businessman had started in 1919.

His father had been a conservative, some say contented, man, whereas the boy had fire in his belly. The first thing the Mogul did was rename the dealership after his daddy. Then he began to do things his way — a big, showy way.

He cranked up the volume of the company's advertising, buying ads in newspapers, radio, and on television. The Mogul was like that politician who was behind in the polls, intent on reaching every single voter who very well might put him over the top. They called him "Mr. Big Volume."[1]

Before the camera he was full of showmanship. He brought a flashy, almost Barnum & Bailey feel to the dealership.

"Customers like excitement," the Mogul said. "They like to shop where business is being done. Nobody likes anything drab."

But behind the scenes he possessed the demeanor of a bean-counter. He would eventually come to wish he'd kept better track of all those beans.

Within the first ten years following his father's death sales reached $30 million. The Mogul bought himself some land and built a fancy flagship showroom and people came from all around to buy cars with reflective chrome wheels and pearlescent paint jobs.

Forbes took notice of the Mogul and named his company to their list of the nation's top 400 privately held businesses. Within two years, the Mogul jumped his company from No. 396 on that list to No. 213. Sales hit $820 million in the mid-1990s. Over 1,500 locals made their living working for the Mogul.

Business far exceeded anything his father had ever done or imagined, still, it wasn't enough. He wanted to be the nation's biggest. He took his brand name on the road and built dealerships in other states. He even gambled on one in Las Vegas.

By 1996, he had expanded his father's humble company into the nation's fifth-ranked auto group. Sales at the Mogul's seven dealerships topped $1 billion that year.

Still it wasn't enough.

"If we have seven more in the right cities, we'll be the No. 1 retailer of cars in the world," said the Mogul.[2]

His goal was to double sales yet again by the year 2000, and he set about doing just that. Sales at his fifteen dealerships topped $2 billion, making his company the world's largest Chevrolet retailer. Along the way, the Mogul earned the praise and envy of his peers far and wide.

He amassed a great fortune and spread it generously around the town that remembered when he was just his father's boy. The city's performing arts theatre bears his name, a nod to the $5 million donation he gave to help build it. He gave to them all — the museums, the schools, the civic clubs, the universities — and in return they gave him their first-born awards.

Still, it wasn't enough. In 2004, at age seventy, he had a castle built for a king. The 28,000-square-foot home sitting on five acres has seven bedrooms, nine full baths, and six half-baths. It is one of largest castles in the county. The Mogul signed a $10 million note for his magnificent new home.

Ahh. The good life. Before long it would all just be a memory fading.

As the business grew, so did the consumer complaints alleging false advertising and deceptive business practices. Customers claimed that they were told they pre-qualified for loans that had never been approved, that dealerships were fishing for customers by sending out advertisements designed to look like recall notices on already-owned vehicles, and that they were advertising mark-downs on cars that they didn't have on their lots.

The Mogul was slapped 113 times in one state for deceptive business practices. The company paid nearly $1 million in penalties for violations in four states.[3]

Sales began to plummet as the nation's economy weakened and the gas prices rocketed. By late August of 2008, the credit market crunched like a tin can under a Silverado's tire. Half of the Mogul's customers had poor credit ratings, many had prior bankruptcies. Their loans came from subprime lenders, often at double-digit interest rates.

On a Wednesday in late September, the Mogul's 2,700 employees awoke to news that they were being laid off, effective immediately. The Repo Man started hauling vehicles off the Mogul's car lots. He filed for chapter 11 bankruptcy. The mansion of his dreams was auctioned off on the courthouse steps. The Mogul that once owned the largest GM dealership in the world owed more than $260 million to 13,000 creditors. Several of his former employees filed lawsuits against him, claiming unfair labor practices. These same employees had been given only a few hours' notice to clear out their offices.

Everything he had worked for from age 27 to 74 was all gone. Unlike his own father he had been neither conservative nor contented. No matter how much he achieved, no matter how much he amassed, it had not been enough. It was never enough.

The Mogul known as Mr. Big Volume has remained mute throughout the collapse of his empire. Castles built of sand never last, no matter how much labor goes into their construction, no matter how magnificent they may seem to onlookers.

Keep in mind the Mogul was a 1950s kid. He grew up in a conservative home in a conservative community, where two RC bottle caps could gain a kid admittance to the movie house on Saturday. He heard the Ten Commandments preached and was taught a strong work ethic. He was no slacker who expected things to be dished up on a silver platter to him.

But somewhere along the way, he got caught up in the relentless pursuit of more. It's almost as if a bad fever came upon him and never abated. If so it's a fever that has afflicted many. It might not be a full-borne plague yet, but it is a blight upon the nation.

At the same time that the Mogul's home was being auctioned off on the courthouse steps, the North American International Auto Show was underway in Detroit.

In November, the CEOs of the nation's leading car dealers — Ford, GM, and Chrysler — had soared into DC on their private jets, begging Congress for a $25 billion handout. They threatened lawmakers that they would have to close their plants and kick their employees to the curb if they didn't get the loan. When word got out to the public that these corporate giants came groveling for public funds on private jets, Congress rebuked them and sent them home with the admonishment to straighten up their act.

They came back the next month, still begging, but this time they came in vehicles, not jets. Congress relented and granted them $13 billion in public aid. But it's difficult to teach an old dog new ways, and the knuckleheads running America's auto industry appear to be particularly reluctant to change. When a National Public Radio correspondent attending that year's trade show asked GM vice-chairman Bob Lutz what it was like to have to depend upon the government's nickel, Lutz responded, "I've never quite been in this situation before of getting a massive pay cut, no bonus, no longer allowed to stay in decent motels, no corporate airplane. I have to stand in line at the Northwest counter," Lutz complained. "I've never quite experienced this before. I'll let you know a year from now what it's like."

Taken aback by Lutz's answer, the befuddled correspondent clarified that he was inquiring about *the company*, not Lutz's personal discomfort.[4] There's good reason why greed is considered one of the seven most deadly sins. Left unbridled, it will destroy all that we build.

THE BOOKSELLER

THE BOOKSELLER WAS WORRIED. WHAT WAS GRANNY going to think? She had built the business from the ground up during a time — the early 1970s — when women in lower Alabama, or in upstate New York, didn't own their own businesses. Yet, over the years, Granny had cultivated a loyal clientele. They came because they loved the feel of linen paper pressed between thumb and forefinger, and for the sacred quiet found between the biographies and the how-to-books. They came for the burst of laughter of a story just told and because they loved the letters marching uniformly across the page. The bookstore brought a sense of order and belonging to their lives. An afternoon spent at the bookstore was like being wrapped in the arms of a beloved aunt, it was a comforting place to linger.

Granny did not woo people with iced mochas or slabs of pound cake or doped-up denizens who greeted fans with false affections. She didn't have to. Granny's charm lies in her belief that everyone is a child of God and she treats them all accordingly, greeting them with hugs and uncommon warmth.

When she was running the shop, Granny knew the stories of her clientele's lives as well as she did the bound ones on the shelves. When their babies got a fever or their mamas were going through the change, she heard about it. When they remodeled the kitchen or tore out the old deck, she heard about that too. If they were vacationing in the Highlands or just headed over to the cabin in DeFuniak Springs, Granny knew. Whatever the life event, Granny knew the perfect book.

Pulling it from among its place in the crowd, she'd hand it over and declare, "You should read this." And they would, simply because they trusted Granny. She wouldn't lead them astray. Many a contented reader has sat with bare feet shoved in the warmth of the coastal sands or on the edge of a weathered pier enjoying the book that Granny recommended. They would forever associate her with the sweet pleasures of their lives.

As a child growing up in Granny's shadow, however, the Bookseller did not understand all that. She had made a promise to herself that as soon as she was able, as soon as she was old enough, as soon as she had enough money, she was going to do one thing for sure — leave town. She had no intentions of taking over Granny's store. Not now. Not e-v-e-r. Nu-huh. No way. No how.

So the Bookseller got herself a degree in high finance. She married a pretty fellow who favored flip-flops and Bermuda shorts. They liked to hike and ski and travel. They liked to hang with friends, sip a little wine, and feel the sun's heat upon their skin.

She got herself a good job in a big bank, in one of those states way out West. She planned to stay there f-o-r-e-v-e-r, working her way up to the corporate boardroom, but then she got preggers and gave birth to a beautiful baby girl and it got her to missing her twin sister so badly. She simply had to return to the place of her own youth, to be near her beloved sissy and the rest of the extended family.

But the bay town was small, corporate jobs sparse. It wasn't as if she could transfer to the corner office of a different firm. She was going to have to forgo her career of high finance and start over, but doing what? Running a shrimp boat? Or a watering hole for the locals, maybe?

"You could buy the bookstore," Sissy suggested.

Oh, brother.

"I didn't picture myself in the business," the Bookseller says. "All throughout my growing up years I'd said never in a million years. It wasn't my passion, but because of my daughter it ended up being everything to me."

She had the acumen and training to run the business. What surprised even her, and delighted everyone else, was just how good she was at the book business.

Granny had not only kept the same clientele, she had kept the same light fixtures, the same shelving, the same flooring.

"Everything was exactly the same as it had been for thirty years," the Bookseller says. "That was part of its charm. Everybody liked that it was the same, but it was dated."

The Bookseller was thirty and hip. She had been to the great beyond and back. There was so much she wanted to do.

"I got ahead of myself," she says. "But that's the thing about successful people, they have this sense of urgency. I wanted to do everything and I wanted to do it today. I'd wake up every morning and couldn't wait to get in to work and accomplish things."

In addition to books, she added a coffee shop and sold the chichi drinks she'd come to love out West. She expanded the stock to include funny cards and trendy trinkets. The kiddy corner became a whole new marketing section. Everything was updated to reflect the young mother's hip style.

"It had an established clientele already but I wanted it to be a place where people of my generation came to as well."

Come they did. The Bookseller knew how to throw a party. When author Fanny Flagg released her book *Can't Wait to Get to Heaven*, the Bookseller found a mansion, filled it with angels, and sent a chariot after Flagg. A thousand people pressed in, hoping to touch the hem of the author's robe.

At the Bookseller's request writers like *The Shack*'s William Young would fly directly from appearances on New York's morning shows to the store by the bay. If she bid them come, they came.

The Bookseller was the Bomb. If she loved a book she could sell hundreds of copies. And best of all? She got to work right alongside Sissy, who owned the frame and art gallery next door.

Life was indescribably good. The kids — there were two daughters now — attended horseback riding and art classes. There was tennis and swimming and late night suppers at The Club. There were also ski vacations and boating adventures.

"I did not think one iota about throwing $100 away. If I had $100, I'd spend it. I told myself that I worked hard, I deserved it."

In 2006 and the start of 2007 business was booming. Sales were up nearly 25 percent over previous years. The Bookseller and her hubby decided it was time to make those home renovations. They took out a second mortgage and planned to get started right after the first of 2007.

Her husband felt uneasy about putting the money they'd borrowed into remodeling the house. There were just too many signs of a slipping economy, he said. They agreed to put their plans on hold until things picked up around the store.

But things didn't pick up, they got worse in a hurry. The Bookseller had to use the money they'd put aside for the house just to keep the business afloat. She went through the budget and made line-item cuts, at work and at home. She jerked back on her purse strings, put the spending on hold. She pulled the kids out of their private lessons and for a couple of months she didn't draw a penny from the business. Still they seemed to be hemorrhaging cash.

"It didn't make any sense," the Bookseller said. "All those years I spent in finance and I couldn't figure out where our money was going. I felt like the stupidest person in the world. It was mind-boggling. I didn't understand what was going wrong."

Granny tried to reassure her. Things will turn around, you'll see. The store has seen lean times before. Not like these, the Bookseller thought. Fearful that they might lose everything, the couple met with an attorney. Granny agreed to loan them her river house so they could put their home up for sale, and, hopefully, get back on their feet financially.

"We talked about filing for bankruptcy. We didn't want to do that but we didn't want to lose our home either," she says. "It seemed to be the time to get out."

Meanwhile, Sissy intervened and signed herself and the Bookseller up for a class with Crown Ministries, a ministry aimed at teaching people how to be financially responsible.

Why not, the Bookseller figured, things couldn't get much worse. The ten-week course was beneficial. Not because it resolved the credit issues. It didn't. During the busiest quarter of the year — the time when a bookstore makes the most profit — half of the Bookseller's major vendors refused to extend her any more credit.

"At that point we were thinking that we might have to take the business out in the woods and shoot it. We realized if it goes under, it goes under. We couldn't keep sinking money into it," she says.

"Because this was a family business, we'd sunk our lives into it. We were doing everything we could for the business, to see it all going away made us feel like we were losing our identity."

But the lessons helped put it all into proper perspective.

"I was stressed but I wasn't nearly as stressed as I normally would be. Because I was in Crown Ministries at the time, I realized even if we lost everything, God will still take care of us."

She felt no shame, no regrets. She had done the best job she knew to do. Whatever happened, she was determined to be at peace with it.

But never in a million years could she have imagined the real reasons for why the business was going under.

For several months the Bookseller had received a late payment notice from one of her credit card companies. She asked her bookkeeper to please call the company and let them know that the bills they kept sending were in error — those balances had been paid.

"We need to talk," her employee said.

"What's up?"

"It's bad news, very bad news. That money that you thought was being used to pay your business card?"

"Yeah?"

"Your former bookkeeper used that money to pay *her* credit card."

"I don't understand."

"She was stealing from you."

"Are you serious?"

"I'm afraid so."

The Bookseller was absolutely floored. That woman, Theresa, had been her friend, her confidant, her gal-pal. Before she quit as the store's bookkeeper in October to take a better job, or so the woman claimed, Theresa had handled all things financial for the Bookseller, even her signature stamp at the bank. Their kids played together. They belonged to the same private country club. How could that woman have betrayed her so?

"At first I didn't understand how bad it was. I thought it meant I might be getting $8,000 back."

"No, that's not what that means," the new bookkeeper said. "There's more."

A lot more. Theresa had used the company's checks to pay tuition for her kids at the private school they attended and swindled funds to pay the country club membership.

Not then, but later, when the depths of the betrayal became clearer, the Bookseller allowed herself a moment of grief.

"I was just so overwhelmed," the Bookseller says, "I cried for five minutes."

It was a Friday in late December when the Bookseller found out about the embezzlement. There were Christmas parties to attend to that weekend, and police to notify come Monday.

"I bet this is the tip of the iceberg," the Bookseller's husband surmised.

It was hard to imagine, but he was right. Police went to Theresa's home in early 2009 and arrested her on twenty-five counts of second-degree possession of a forged instrument. All-in-all she had allegedly pilfered $150,000 from the store by the bay. The FBI is involved, but whether or not the Bookseller will ever recoup monies lost is undetermined.[1]

Sure, the Bookseller is angry, but she's determined to find a way to forgive even this.

"We may never get a penny of restitution and yes, that will upset me — I want justice — but I will forgive this."

But such forgiveness is a day-to-day, moment-to-moment decision.

"Sometimes I can't believe it happened, but mostly I look at it as a chapter in our lives, and our lives are so full we don't dwell on it."

Sometimes it makes a person angrier to watch a loved one go through a difficult situation than they would be to go through it themselves. Granny was oh-so-very mad and hurt when she learned how that woman had taken advantage of the Bookseller.

"I was full of emotions, but then, while doing my Bible lesson, something would jump out at me," Granny says.

Words of comfort like, "Be still and know that I am your God."

And words of admonishment. "Pray for your enemies."

"I realized I had to let go of my anger and trust in the Lord," says Granny. "Some of the best lessons in life are learned the hard way and I've had my share. I do have faith in the Lord."

She also has faith in her granddaughter. Granny knows that the Bookseller will come away from this a better woman. Since discovering the theft and the reason for the cash loss, the business has turned a corner.

"It's amazing how fast things have turned around since we found the cancer and stopped it," the Bookseller says. "Things are still scary right now but the people that I've talked to who have been through this said things would continue to turn fast."

All-in-all she thinks it's a blessing, really.

"Not because of the embezzlement, but because I've learned that this business isn't my identity — the business is my ministry. It's family, first and foremost, that defines me."

Like many, that woman grew up in a culture of "get it now and pay later." That kind of culture creates desperate people. It was greed that led the boy Edmund in C. S. Lewis's *The Lion, the Witch and the Wardrobe*, to betray his siblings. Once he'd tasted the Turkish delight, Edmund could never get enough of it. It was a relentless hungering for that which he already had.

Greed causes people of all ages and all backgrounds to betray their best pals — and, sometimes, to swindle away the Savior himself.

THE JUBILEE

THE RINGING STARTLED ME. I GRABBED MY CELL PHONE and looked at the time. It was 5:45 a.m. in Fairhope, Alabama. I didn't recognize the number of the incoming call but I answered it anyway.

"Karen, Jubilee," a voice whispered.

★

I popped up out of that bed faster than if a rattler had just bit me.

It had been a week to the day since I first learned of the Jubilee. An artist told me about it over dinner of shrimp and grits.

"Nobody knows when they'll happen or even why they happen," she said. "But some of the old seers know when they are going to happen. They say the air turns silky, and it blows from the east."

Or the north, others claim.

"Promise you'll call me, if you see one coming," I begged.

I made everyone promise me that. The artist. The ladies at book club. The writers group that meets at the cottage on Tuesdays.

"Have you ever seen a Jubilee?" I asked the sales clerk at a dry goods store.

"Only once," she said.

"What was it like?" I asked.

"It was three a.m. My husband called me. I went down to the bay in a hurry."

"Have you seen a Jubilee?" I asked a computer technician.

"Lived here fifteen years and I've never seen one," he said.

"And you?" I asked the librarian. "Have you seen one?"

"No," she said. "You have to be on somebody's call list."

"How do I get on that call list?" I asked my friend Joe.

"Well, you have to know someone who lives along the bay and they have to be willing to call. There are people who've lived here all their lives and never seen one."

"I have to see one," I said. "I have to get on that call list."

★

"Who is this?" I asked as I began fumbling around for my contact case. I couldn't see a whale in the living room without my contacts or glasses.

"It's Donna Hill from book club," she replied. "Hurry and get on down here. It's a Jubilee."

Some Jubilees only last an hour or two. Donna had waited nearly an hour already before calling, unsure as to whether she ought to wake me or not. Although I'd assured her and everyone else that I've been woken at two a.m. for fires, for murders, for car wrecks, and for babies puking. Please. If you ever hear that one of God's great mysteries is unfolding at two a.m., please, please call me.

I still didn't have my contacts in but I scribbled Donna's address on the palm of my hand. Then I put my lenses in, pulled on a shirt and a pair of shorts, grabbed a ball cap, and ran out the door. I called my husband on my way. It was four a.m. in Oregon.

"Tim, there's a Jubilee," I whispered.

"Oh, wow!" he whispered back. Then I burst into tears and ran the red light, afraid I'd miss it, this phenomenon of nature.

It took me fifteen minutes to reach the Hills' home in Point Clear. Donna was waiting for me at the front door with a coffee cup in hand. Donna is a blonder version of Beth Moore. Petite and always impeccably dressed in that way of a southern woman who instinctively knows when it's okay to wear flip-flops and when to wear the stilettos, and looks great in either. She offered me the cup, slipped on her flip-flops, and out the back door we went.

Unaware that a Jubilee was imminent, Donna's neighbors, Frank and Jane Feagin, had left their crab traps out all night long. The traps were nearly full. The Feagins planned to shell the crabs later that day in anticipation of company coming in for the weekend. But when Frank realized there was a Jubilee underway, he yanked up his traps. Dozens of crustaceans were all dead, like hardened sailors trapped in a submarine that failed and sunk to the airless deep.

Frank was trying painstakingly to scoop up what shrimp he could with a net but this was primarily a flounder Jubilee.

"Get your gig," Donna instructed. "Leon and Mr. Pate are catching them down there." She pointed to shallow waters three piers down, where there were swirls of fish heading. Leon, Donna's husband, and Mr. Pate, a neighbor, carried buckets brimming with fish. It looked as though somebody dumped a gym bag full of ping-pong paddles into the warm gray waters of Point Clear. Schools of flat flounder flopped on their sides, striving to get oxygen into their gills.

Frank and I climbed down the pilings, waded out into the knee-deep waters, carefully searching for firm footing on pillows of sand. Me with a bucket. Frank with a gig. Muscular eel swam between my legs. The flounder made flapping noises reminiscent of a scene from Hitchcock's *The Birds* as they tried frantically to suck air, to draw breath.

"There's one," I shouted, pointing to a particularly sizable flounder. Frank held the gig's wooden handle steady, aimed the pointy-steel end, and drove it into the fish's middle. I held out the plastic bucket and Frank plopped the fish in. Jane leaned over the pilings and excitedly pointed to another. Then another. I felt like a six-year-old locked unexpectedly in a candy store overnight. There were fish every which way we looked. All ours for the taking. I was awestruck. I'd never seen such bounty of fish before. I uttered prayers of thankfulness. I didn't know why I'd been one of the Jubilee's Chosen, but Almighty God, was I ever thankful that I was one.

Neighbors motored their boats alongside us, carrying gigs and buckets and nets of their own. We took our share and then some, filling buckets and boats with all manner of fish. At eight a.m. we took our flounder back to the Feagins' pier. Frank and I had gigged forty total, all of them big as a silver tray, plenty large enough to feed the multitudes. We spread them out on the buffet table at the pier and took pictures. Frank took to skinning them, and Jane said come Friday night we'd have us a big feast.

In the old days, people would come from miles around for a Jubilee. Someone in the community would ring loud bells whenever the fish started rising. People would come to the bay with their buckets and coolers, gigs and nets, and gather more fish than they ever imagined. Leon once took in fifty flounder during one Jubilee but decided that was just too much for one man to clean. He stopped at thirty this time round.

Locals say there are only two places in the world where Jubilees happen — Mobile Bay, which the Spaniards named The Bay of the Holy Spirit, and Tokyo Bay, only you can't eat the fish out of Tokyo Bay because of the mercury levels. The name, Jubilee, refers to the abundant bounty provided by an act of nature.

Scientists have kind of figured out the mechanics of a Jubilee. They know what happens — oxygen levels in the water drop so drastically that the bottom fish rise to the surface seeking air. Flounder. Shrimp. Crab. Eel. They head for shallow waters, or beach themselves, in desperate search of air.

What the experts haven't yet deciphered is what causes the oxygen levels to drop and why sometimes the only fish to surface are shrimp or sometimes only flounder or sometimes only crab. But it's jarring to realize that the thing that creates so much exhilaration among land-crawlers is the very thing that leaves hundreds, sometimes thousands of fish, beached and dead.

After all the fish were cleaned, I drove back into Fairhope, straight to the home of Stacey Howell, my friend who had hosted the book club luncheon where I'd met Donna Hill and Jane Feagin. Had it not been for Stacey I would have missed the Jubilee. Stacey had been frantically trying to reach me all morning long. She was afraid I'd missed it but as soon as she opened the door to her Bay Street home, she knew differently.

"Oh, Stacey," I said and burst into tears. Then my beautiful, generous friend took me by the hand, pulled me into the house and laughed and cried with me the kind of tears which only the joy of pure things can elicit.

Being part of a Jubilee is not something to be taken for

granted. I knew that then as I recounted the morning's events for Stacey, but I understood it even better that evening while sleeping out on Frank and Jane Feagin's pier.

Frank has old Army bunkbeds that he's set up on his pier. Sometimes, on comfortable nights, he and Jane will sleep out there, under the stars, listening to the seagulls bark and the neighbors' chatter. They'd graciously invited me to come back that night to sleep out on the Bay of the Holy Spirit.

I didn't get back to their place until well after dark. They were gone, off to pick up their son who was flying in from D.C. I climbed on the bottom bunk and read for awhile, then eased my way down the steps to the short dock that stretched out into the silvery waters. A Kenny Chesney tune floated past. Somebody, somewhere had left a radio on.

Shining the flashlight that Frank had left with me into the murky bay waters, I spotted what looked like the cast-off limb of a Civil War ghost-soldier floating past. I moved closer to the dock's edge and, holding on to a rail, leaned out over the water.

Oh. It was only an eel. Bloated and eerily white from death.

I flashed the light to the other side of the dock.

A fluorescent white blob bobbed by me. It was a flounder. Larger than any I'd seen all day. It was huge. The size of three of our biggest flounders.

I climbed up the steps, back to the place where Frank had shown me the switch to the flood lights and turned them on. Then I bent over the railing and could not believe what I saw. It looked like somebody had turned over a truck of fish, right off the end of the pier.

The remains of that morning's Jubilee circled me, like some ancient ritual where the dead, white and bloated, gathered to cry out: Why did so many of us have to sacrifice for the benefit of so few?

That's how it is with any Jubilee though, isn't it?

Talk about your law of the universe. Here's one you can write down on the palm of your hand and on the doorpost of your home: One person's jubilation over abundance almost always comes at the expense of somebody else's sacrifice.

That's the way it is. We don't have to beat ourselves up over that. It would be just as great a sin to not be thankful when the Jubilee comes our way as it is to swindle folks out of their hard-earned money.

Money is not the problem.

We are.

We are not satisfied with one 12,000-square-foot home. We have to have two of them. We are so busy wishing for a double-wide that we forget the shelter and security that a single-wide provides. We are so concerned about trying to bring in the biggest haul that we completely miss out on the joy of the abundance God has already given to us.

THE MARINE

COLLARDS STEEP ON THE DASHBOARD IN A TUPPERWARE container as Miz Betty rests her arms on the steering wheel of the Astro van. Coarse gray hair falls in chunky curls around her shoulders. She pulls a length of brown yarn from a skein.

"Good Morning, Betty," the Marine says. "You knitting another afghan?"

"Crocheting," she says, correcting the fellow with the red goatee and shaved head. Knotty-fuzz blankets are wrapped around her stumpy legs and her fleshy bottom insulating her against the chill of a fading winter morning.

She puts the yarn aside and cuts her blue eyes at the folks gathered around her front door. For the past four years, Miz Betty's vehicle has been her home. The van rocks as if someone's pushing it from the other side.

"That's my son," Miz Betty explains. "He just woke up."

The man is fully dressed in jeans and a plaid shirt when he plops down in the passenger seat and lights up a smoke. Miz Betty sells cigarettes for a quarter apiece right here from her front door. It is one of the ways the sixty-five-year-old woman can make a little extra cash.

The city recently ticketed Miz Betty for selling stuff from

her van without a vendor's license. That's one of the ways that life on the streets is so tough. Homeless folks like Miz Betty get a bad rap for being shiftless. "Get a job" is the mantra of those who have to those who have not. But whenever someone like Miz Betty figures out a decent way to make a dollar, some official comes along and devises a way to take it from her.

So Miz Betty gives away a lot of stuff too.

"I give out whatever it is they need if I've got more than one."

From the looks of the van, she's got more dry goods than a dollar store. There's pens, paper, books, blankets, socks, jeans, coats, boots, bags of cookies, crackers, and for today, collards, fatback, and pinto beans for lunch. There's even a porta-potty in the back, somewhere underneath the bags of clothes and remnants of another life.

She grew up on a tobacco farm and learned to cook biscuits and cornbread from scratch.

"By the time I was eight I was cooking for all the farm hands," she says.

When she was a young woman, Miz Betty never imagined that one day she might be living on the streets of this sunny city where she's lived her whole life long.

"When I was thirty, my plans were a whole lot bigger than this," she says.

She married a Korean War veteran and raised some children. They had a decent life, until her husband fell from a nine-story building. Amazingly he survived the fall, only to die not too much later from cancer. His medical bills were covered but there was no life insurance. Miz Betty says she sold the double-wide home he'd bought her so she could give him a decent burial.

"He was a war veteran, I thought he deserved it," she says. "I didn't want the state just throwing him in a ditch somewhere."

The funeral cost her $4,000. She bought a single-wide with the leftover cash. They have rules in those mobile home parks, though. Rules that Miz Betty couldn't always abide by. The manager and Miz Betty couldn't get along. She told Miz Betty to hook that trailer up to a rig and get a move on down the road.

"Things just started going downhill," Miz Betty says.

She didn't have the money necessary to move the trailer. So she just loaded what she could into her vehicle and drove away from the trailer park.

She doesn't blame God for her situation. It isn't his fault. It's purely a money matter.

"I don't have any," Miz Betty says by way of explanation.

She gets a government check once a month. It's something, but not enough. If a person wants to move into a decent place, something safe, they need to have about $3,000 in savings. Enough to cover first and last month's rent and a security deposit. Miz Betty doesn't have that kind of cash flow.

Some of the church folks who help with the homeless got Miz Betty an apartment. They moved her into it but for whatever reason, it didn't suit her. Miz Betty told some that it's because the apartment was in a dangerous part of town. She felt safer in her vehicle.

The worst thing about living in a van is the same thing about living most anywhere, there's never enough storage space.

"It's cramped. Just like living in a camper," she says. "It's hard but you do what you have to do to survive."

Not to romanticize the street life, but Miz Betty's life has purpose. Her van is the trading post of this homeless community. It is one of the places they gather to get the day's news, to catch up on each other, to buy cheap cigarettes.

"If Miz Betty wasn't here, she'd be in a Barcalounger

watching Oprah," says the Marine. "To her, this makes sense. Her life has purpose. She matters here."

Miz Betty passes the day by crocheting and reading. She pulls a paperback book from the dash.

"I like Christian fiction. Debbie Macomber is my favorite."

Must be that crocheting and knitting thing the two women share. That and their faith.

"You have to have hope and faith," Miz Betty says. "If you don't have that you don't have anything."

She doesn't bother to ask God why she's in the fix she's in. Miz Betty prefers to focus on the constructive.

"I ask him what he has in store for me now that I'm here."

★

The homeless and their friends gather at the park near the bus station, the park with the metal acorn at its center. This is their gathering place. This is their living room, where they lounge on park benches or stand underneath the oaks and discuss the state of things.

The Marine sets up a table. The Biscuit Lady pulls out the warmer. Suzanne unloads bags of fresh laundry. Greg sets out the hot coffee and the sugar. The homeless are picky about their coffee.

"If you can see the bottom of the cup through the coffee, I don't want it," Michael says.

It won't be strong enough, and it's got to have plenty of sugar.

"I'm that guy who gets fifteen packs of sugar for one cup."

Michael wears a blue satin baseball jacket, the sort that's popular with high schoolers. He's not all that much of a baseball fan, but the coat is warm, and warmth matters on the streets. He's looking for work. Landscaping, hopefully.

"It's almost spring and I like being outside," he says. He's fifty and has an eye that's turned bad, cataracts or a street fight perhaps, it's hard to tell. But otherwise, he could pass for someone ten years younger.

"I always tell people you've got to take care of yourself."

Lena tells them that too. For far too many years, she didn't take care of herself, but she's been sober two years now. She's fifty-nine and has liver disease. The last time she ended up at Dorthea Dix Hospital the doctors told her that if she came in again it would be to the morgue. Sure enough, that was a sobering thought.

When Lena first met the Marine she was going through a tough time. She was short on cash and behind on her light bill. She asked the Marine if he could spot her for it. He told her no, he didn't have the means to help her out. Lena was mad.

"I thought you were my friend," she said.

"I am."

"Then why won't you help me out?" she implored.

Lena assumed he had the money to fix her problem but was simply too stingy to do so. She didn't know his story. Didn't know how it was that this white-bread Marine with the closet full of Hugo Boss suits ended up in the living room underneath the oaks.

"Tell you what I'll do, Lena," the Marine said. "I can't keep the power company from turning your lights off, but I will come sit with you in the dark after they turn them off."

He meant it too.

"I think that's what Jesus does — he sits with us in the dark," says the Marine.

★

He joined the Marines out of high school. The military provided the quickest escape route out of rural Mississippi. He doesn't sugarcoat his childhood.

"I grew up white trash."

His father was an appliance repair guy. His mom stayed home to raise the couple's three boys. They lived in a Jim Walter home.

"It was 1,100 square feet with masonite siding and a 10-percent fixed-rate mortgage. Affluence hit our family when Mom got a job at Walmart. We could afford new clothes then."

He became the family bookworm; reading gave him access to a lifestyle of finely crafted leather shoes and tailored suits. He grew up wanting one thing — to be rich. Gordon Gekko was his hero. The "Greed is Good" character in the flick *Wall Street*.

"I was that guy who thought the best thing I could do for the poor was not become one of them," the Marine says.

He sits outside a Starbucks, sans sunglasses even on this bright day, his blue eyes squinting. He's dressed warmly in a sweatshirt and jeans, topped with a functional khaki jacket, not North Face or Columbia, but something of equal quality and suitable purpose. He sips a cup of coffee, black.

He leans forward over the wrought-iron table and tells his own story logically, chronologically, easily, a man with no bones to hide now that so much life has passed. He's thirty-six.

He had the smarts for college and the scholarships too. But in his neighborhood, if a fellow wanted to be respected he went into the service. College was for pansies. So he joined the Marines and earned his stripes, and after he finished up with that, he began to pursue his dream.

"I wanted to be a millionaire by the time I was thirty-five."

He read all the right books and stood in front of the mirror every morning repeating, "I am a money magnet. Money is attracted to me." Seriously. He did that.

"I had that whole law of attraction thing down — if you think rich, you'll be rich."

On a lark, he went with a friend to take the test to become a fireman. He passed, his friend didn't.

"I guess God told them to hire me and not him," he says, laughing, not the least bit serious.

Firefighting wasn't going to make him rich, but that chick he met at the bar, now she could, or at least her daddy could. Her daddy was a rich man.

"I remember the first time I went to her home to pick her up. They had an 8,000-square-foot house. They'd just downsized. The doorbell had a speaker, an intercom system. It was the first time I'd ever seen one of those."

If her family suspected him of being white trash, they never said. They were welcoming, embracing. He fell in love with the family and with their lifestyle.

"I'm going to date myself here but it was just like *Dallas*, the TV show. There was this patriarch, and everyone gathered around him. I fell in love with that. The marriage was a match made in hell."

Firefighting led to a job selling life insurance which led him to a job as a financial planner. It was all part of the bigger picture. Every friend he made, every barbecue he attended, every donation he gave, be it monetary or the gift of time, was all calculated. From his suits, with their Ermenegildo Zegna ties, to which neighborhood he lived in — a gated community — to which church he attended — the megachurch better for networking — was all about playing the part of the wannabe. By age twenty-seven he was pulling down nearly six figures a year.

But making money wasn't as fulfilling as he'd first imagined it would be. He recalled a conversation he had with a client he'd culled from his network at church.

"She called me one day and said, 'All my problems are solved! Jesus sent me a pre-approved Visa card with a $10,000 credit limit! Isn't that great?"

He couldn't believe what he was hearing. Did she really believe that Jesus had sent her a credit card? All that reading he'd done as a young boy made him a thinker. Much as he wanted otherwise, he just didn't have what it took to be a rabid consumer.

It was while participating in the spiritual renewal program, The Walk to Emmaus, that the Marine decided to change his life's course. But his even participating in The Walk was solely because it was a necessary step to becoming more high-profile in the corporate structure of his church.

"I didn't sign up for spiritual growth. I wanted to be seen and recognized as the money man in church," he says.

He failed to take into consideration the power of the Holy Spirit, however. It was while sitting in a dark, silent sanctuary that he began to see that his life had been all about him. His marriage. His job. His friends. Words from the praise song "Heart of Worship" were on replay in his head: "I'm sorry Lord for the thing I've made it. When it's all about You."

He'd lived by a Creed of Greed. If a relationship couldn't be exploited to better his position in life, what good was it? He was a greedy son-of-a-gun and up until that very moment had been proud of that.

"I was a fraud," the Marine says. "My marriage was falling apart. I was $30,000 in debt. And I didn't want to help rich old white people hide their money from the government anymore."

He grew weary of the hunt, hung up his suits, and bought a used bookstore in Memphis. A bookstore is a great way to go broke slowly, he says.

"You make enough money to pay the bills and give you hope that you might make money the next year."

Not long afterwards, the little woman walked out on him. The Marine was the first in his family to divorce, and that alone was cause enough to make him question who he really was underneath that Glossy-God-Man exterior. He began to read Dietrich Bonhoeffer, Thomas Merton, and Dorothy Day. The Marine refers to the bookstore as a four-year detox.

"I had to learn to be okay with not being a success. I had to detox from money and that whole culture of greed."

He made new friends. Real friends.

"They weren't people I could exploit. I didn't need them as potential prospects to sell things to. They were just friends."

He began to discover a whole new depth to his faith. The more he read, the more the Marine contemplated, what about the poor? Day wrote that she firmly believed salvation depended upon the poor. Merton noted, "It is easy enough to tell the poor to accept their poverty as God's will when you yourself have warm clothes and plenty of food and medical care and a roof over your head and no worry about the rent. But if you want them to believe you — try to share some of their poverty and see if you can accept it as God's will for yourself!"[1] And Mother Teresa said, "The most terrible poverty is loneliness and the feeling of being unloved." Of all the issues of his day, Jesus spoke most often of the poor. Why?

It was his contemplation over these matters that compelled the Marine to sell off the bookstore and move out of Memphis.

"Before I was that guy who was completely convinced that

Jesus was in full support of laissez-faire capitalism, but all that reading starts to mess with your head."

The Marine rubs a palm over the stubble of hair and laughs at the man he used to be. He's been in the city where Miz Betty grew up nearly two years now. He's what you call an urban preacher. He heads up Love Wins Ministries.

It's not your typical ministry. There's no church building. No deacons. No creed, per se. There is a website (http://lovewins. info) and there are a handful of donors. Most give less than $50 a month. The Marine lives on less than many of the street people he's trying to befriend.

He's loathe to say he ministers to the homeless. That would imply that he's in some elevated position over others, instead of being a part of the community of the homeless. What he and the others involved in Love Wins Ministry do is provide the most practical of help to the homeless.

When the homeless are bleeding, the Marine goes with them to the hospital and sits with them in the emergency room. When their eyeglasses are broken, the Marine takes them to the place where they can get a whole new pair for $5. Someone in the ministry buys them steel-toed boots because a fellow who has those boots can get hired as a day laborer in construction. That job will pay him $75 a day, versus those who don't have the regulatory boots and can only work jobs that pay $40 a day. Despite the stereotype of being shiftless no-counts, the Marine insists that many of the homeless are hard workers. He eats with them, he laughs with them, he argues politics and religion with them, and sometimes he holds them as they both cry over their inability to rise above all this.

If the Marine had a goal posted to his mirror today, which

he doesn't, it would say something about being the hands and feet of Jesus.

"This came about because of some tugging on my heart that I ought to be doing more for the poor, not because I'm doing some penance for my twenties," he says.

He came to the city pretty much the same way many homeless come to any city, without a job, and without a place to sleep. It was a little discombobulating at first, trying to figure out what a ministry to the poor ought to look like. The only thing for sure that he knew was that he didn't want to be in a position that separated him from them. He wanted to do just as he told Lena he would do — sit with them in their darkness.

So he decided to take the skills he'd learned in the corporate world and build a network within the homeless community. Instead of working behind the warming pans in the soup kitchen, he took a bowl of whatever it was they were eating and ate beside them. In a sense, he became one of them, sharing in their afflictions and in their comforts.

Ronnie, one of the homeless, was ticketed by a city cop for sleeping on a park bench. The fine was $110. If Ronnie had that kind of money to waste he probably wouldn't have been sleeping in the city park to begin with. The Marine told Ronnie he'd go to court with him.

The Marine showed up in court dressed to the nines in the armor of his former life, one of those $800 suits. He had a chat with the DA about how ridiculous a notion it is to fine the homeless for being, well, homeless. The DA agreed. They threw out Ronnie's ticket. Ronnie was elated. He told everybody he knew that the Marine was a freaking Perry Mason. The Marine was their friend. The Marine was somebody who really cared. The Marine was the Bomb. The Marine was the Man.

★

The homeless could teach churches and cities a thing or two about how to build community. When you live on the streets, you learn to look out for each other. When everything you own fits into three bags, you need to be able to trust somebody to watch over your property. The homeless know how to be good neighbors. Like us, they don't always do it, but they know how.

The Biscuit Lady and her husband remember that first Sunday they came down to the park with the acorn at its center. Their interest in the homeless was more personal than most. The Biscuit Lady's kid brother lived on the streets of Tacoma for twenty-five years.

Like every homeless person, there's a convoluted story behind how he got there. He'd grown up in a good home, well-loved, and went off to one of them highfalutin and high price-tag Christian colleges and earned himself a piece of parchment paper and a degree in one of the "ologies." He got married and had a kid. Then he started drinking, socially, then more than that. Anyway, he's the reason the Biscuit Lady and her husband, a retired IBM guru, got involved.

Like the Marine, they just decided they'd wing it. They didn't get city permits or hook up with any organization. They simply came one cold misty morning with a couple of gallons of hot coffee and fresh-from-the-oven biscuits.

They picked a corner near the bus station, parked their vehicle, set up a table and unloaded the goods, then stood around waiting for the homeless to turn out in droves. No one came.

"I felt foolish," says the Biscuit Lady's husband. "We had forty-eight biscuits. I figured we'd end up taking every single one of them home."

It was a pretty misty morning, so it was hard to see across the street to the park. Where were all the homeless? He spotted one fellow hunkered down next to a nearby building. He poured two cups of coffee, one for himself and one for the other guy. He walked it over and said, "Would you like a cup of coffee?"

"Sure would," came the answer.

And then moments later, the table was surrounded by the hungry and homeless. The biscuits and coffee were gone, completely. It was as if that man had tapped out some secret code that reverberated up and down the streets of the Acorn city, telling others that it was okay, that the Biscuit Lady and her husband were harmless. Yes. The homeless worry about us, the same way we worry about them.

"People think of us as being harmful," says Michael, the fellow in the baseball jacket. "We're not harmful. But they don't like it if we run to a table. I guess if we're running they think we're going to rob them or something."

The Biscuit Lady's husband laughs at the truth of that. Unless it's up and down a court, or around an asphalt track, white people are afraid of black men running. Even if it's just a cup of hot coffee that's got them on the run.

The Marine isn't black and he's not poor really.

"I could never be poor in the same way these people are. By virtue of my education and skin color I have options they would never dream of. Poverty is, more than anything, a lack of choice," the Marine explains.

He adds that the homeless understand community in a way that many of us don't because they have to.

"You and I do not need community," the Marine says. "We have privilege. We have education. We have money. We were born white and in America, which means we won the lottery.

The homeless must have community in order to survive. The saddest thing to see is when one of them gets shunned by the others. It really can mean the difference between survival and not."

When we want to go out and get food, we can lock our doors and turn on our home alarms to protect our property. The homeless have to ask the help of a neighbor.

"Hey man, can you watch my stuff while I get through that line?"

We have safety deposit boxes and bank accounts. When somebody writes us a check, we deposit it in the bank. The poor can't afford an account. Should they be so fortunate as to have someone scribble out a check to them, they have to take the check to the bank it was written upon and then pay a fee to have that check cashed.

The system is designed to make poor people poorer and rich people richer. Lena or Ronnie might have to pay upwards of $15 to get a $100 check cashed. That might be a tenth of the income they take home for the week. That fee goes toward paying that $25 million in annual salaries those corporate heads rake in.

That's the thing with a lot of the homeless. They aren't crooks like these corporate heads. Unlike Bernie Madoff or those slick-talking prosperity evangelists, they aren't trying to cheat anybody. They are just trying to stay warm for another day.

Life has beat them with their own bootstraps. They're not resilient, they're resigned. They don't have the wherewithal to argue with the phone company or the bank teller or the light company. So they sit in the dark. And if they are very, very lucky, they have a friend like the Marine or the Biscuit Lady to sit with them.

A lot of us want to help the poor on our own terms. We want to give them a home in the burbs and a big-screen plasma TV because we believe that is the American Dream. We think that if only they had Jesus they wouldn't be the way they are, they'd be like us. We Christians are bad that way. We treat people like they are paper dolls. We want to paste cut-out clothes and shoes on them and display them on our refrigerator doors.

So we donate our dollars to downtown missions and pray that they will be successful at getting people like Ronnie and Michael and Miz Betty off the streets. It never occurs to us that these people aren't lost. They are just poor.

We make the poor gather in circles and hold hands to pray. Or we put them in a room and preach to them for forty-five minutes before we feed them. That paradigm seems twisted to the Marine.

"We don't feed the homeless so that we can preach the gospel to them," he says. "We feed them because that is the gospel."

★

Vernon is a scrawny veteran with a steel-rod in a bum leg and a black knit cap on his head. When he has a little bit of money he lives in a rental. When he doesn't he lives under the overpass or wherever else it is he can escape the elements, be it rain or a steaming sun.

"What are you writing?" he asks.

"A book."

"What's the name of it?"

"*Will Jesus Buy Me a Double-Wide?*"

Scooching in close enough to whisper, Vernon says, "Tell Jesus to buy you two so you can give one to ol' Vernon."

★

Listen up all you prosperity pimps. God is not a capitalist. He's not our broker. He's not our wizard or personal shopping assistant. His love for us cannot be measured by the number of cars in our garage or how many Jimmy Choo heels are in our closets. To suggest that any of the material blessings we enjoy are the result of our merit or our faithfulness is outright foolishness.

"That's throwing grace to hell out the window," says the Marine.

Such perverted theology angers him.

"We think in America that the good job, the promotion, the house, the new car, that God gave them to us because he loves us. We are in his good graces, a chosen people, a 'Christian nation,' and he proves that by 'blessing us.' That works fine as long as everything goes great. But when the crap hits the fan, when we lose the job, when the husband runs off with the secretary, when we get cancer, or our kid is killed in a car wreck, now what? Does this mean God does not love us anymore? Our easy God is gone and we are screwed like a rabbit in the springtime."

The Marine sums up Christianity this way: "Go love somebody who can't love you back. Love somebody who can't do anything for you. Get off your butt and love somebody who can't benefit you in any way. Somebody who is never going to repay you. They are never going to invite you over to eat at their house. That's the gospel. Not God loves you and has a wonderful plan for your life which includes a Mercedes Benz, a corner office, and a secretary with fake boobs."

Amen. Amen. And Amen.

★

Being Homeless
Hugh Hollowell

Being homeless means wearing clothes you did not pick out.

Being homeless means eating what they give you.

Being homeless means having to hear a sermon before you can eat.

Being homeless means being asked for your ID by the police for being in the park.

Being homeless means hiding everything you own so no one will throw it away.

Being homeless means spending most of your day with addicts and the mentally ill, even if you yourself are not.

Being homeless means people are surprised you have an opinion on the presidential election.

Being homeless means walking several miles to eat.

Being homeless means you hope the crazy street preachers show up because it is Saturday and the soup kitchens are closed.

Being homeless means eating meals in a soup kitchen no person would ever order in a restaurant.

Being homeless means chicken hot dogs.

Being homeless means hearing people tell you you should be thankful for what you get (like chicken hot dogs).

Being homeless means rich church folks giving you secondhand underwear.

Being homeless means standing in line for everything.

Being homeless means paying 25 cents to pee.

Being homeless means crying when it rains because you know everything you own is ruined.

Being homeless means having to choose between staying in the shelter tonight or going to work today.

Being homeless means going to the day labor place at 3 a.m. and signing in so you can work that day and make $47.

Being homeless means paying $5 to cash that $47 check.

Being homeless means you are supposed to be thankful the county will let six of you take a shower each week. During the day. When you could be looking for a job.

Being homeless means being called ungrateful when you ask why only six, when there are 2000 homeless in the county.

Being homeless means wondering how you are supposed to get a job when you cannot take a shower.

Being homeless means being thankful when the temperature drops below 32 degrees because it means you are allowed in the shelter that night.

Being homeless means trying not to ask yourself if there is really a difference between sleeping outside when it is 32 degrees and when it is 35 degrees.

Being homeless means people will judge you for smoking cigarettes.

Being homeless means being afraid to tell anyone where you sleep.

Being homeless means talking to your children on a borrowed phone.

Being homeless means being afraid to hope anymore.

THE PREACHER

THE GOSPEL OF ENTITLEMENT IS PREACHED FROM A platform in a downtown arena and over fifty thousand flock to hear it. They want to believe, as their pastor does, that God is going to prosper them.

"God wants to increase you financially," he said.

All you have to do is believe.

Have enough faith.

Change your way of thinking.

Quit being so negative all the time.

Hop out of bed in the morning and go about your day expecting people to go out of their way to help you. Expect the favor of God upon your lives.

You deserve better than you are getting. You, after all, are God's chosen. The ones he loves.

And how does God express that love?

By showering us with lavish lifestyles. Bigger houses. Bigger paychecks. Bigger cars. Bigger stadiums. Bigger churches. Maybe even bigger Bibles, preferably ones that come with amortization charts.

Preacher Smiley tells of the day he and his beautiful wife were out walking the neighborhood and came upon a big mansion, just like the pink, two-story one where Barbie and Ken shack up, only this one wasn't made of plastic. It was made of marble and fine crown molding. His wife wanted the big house. It would be hers to have, if only he had as much faith as she did.

But he didn't.

"That home is so far beyond our reach," he told his bride.

But she didn't listen. Instead, she began praying for that house, for God's favor, for the entitlement of the Chosen. She told her husband they would have a house like that someday. Maybe one even bigger, even better.

It is, after all, the American way.

God's will for his beloved children.

Fortunately, she had enough faith for the both of them.

"She kept speaking words of victory and faith," he recalled, "and she finally talked me into it."

That's what Preacher Smiley calls living by the Word of Faith.

Other husbands, with a more secular bent, simply call it being nagged to death. Such men are rarely as rich as Preacher Smiley and his picture-perfect wife. Preacher Smiley would probably look at the Mayor's life and pity him. So much potential gone to seed. The Mayor greets each day with gratitude. He's thankful to have lived another day. But he doesn't rise up in the mornings and expect to put his bare feet down on a red carpet. Mayor prefers the cold hardwood floor.

The Mayor does not go about his day imagining what wonderful blessings his good neighbors will shower upon him. Mayor doesn't expect anyone to do anything for him but he's always happy when they do. He's happy when they don't too. Mayor has learned to be contented, with or without, the way the apostle Paul spoke of.

It's almost anti-Christian and un-American to be contented

anymore. A whole slew of believers think that faith is measured in dollars and cars. The more faith you have the more consumer goods there are to show for it.

Don't accept the status quo, Preacher Smiley said. Don't be mediocre. Be a better you. Be richer, smarter, healthier, more successful in every way than your parents were and their parents before them.

There's not much mention of being more godly. The g-word has lost favor with God's people. It's hard to feel empowered when the standard for godliness is Jesus Christ. Jesus was one of the Chosen. In fact, he was *The* Chosen. But his mandate on earth didn't have a thing to do with riches, wealth, or prospering in any fashion. He came to serve. His mission was to be a living sacrifice for our sins. Sins like our greed. Our selfishness. Our ambition. While we go in search of God's favor every day, Jesus seems to have lost favor with us.

The few times Jesus is referred to in these bestselling give-it-to-me-right-this-minute-God books, he is touted as being a wealthy man.

"He looked successful and He acted successful. He dressed as a successful person. His clothing was so valuable that even at his crucifixion the Roman soldiers would not cut it up."[1]

Preacher Smiley says that Christ's crucifixion is the victory we need to quit living our barely-get-by-lives. Because of the price Christ paid, we have *the right* to live in total victory. Partial victory means we have a good family and good health but we constantly struggle with finances. That's not good enough. That's not total victory. Get a vision for it. Preferably one with dollar signs.

People who don't envision themselves as wealthy rarely are. That's what all the prosperity teachers teach. The ones who believe in Jesus as their personal Lord and Savior and those who don't.

A person doesn't have to be a Christian to be a devotee of the Gospel of Entitlement. You don't have to believe in God or in his favor. You only have to believe that you deserve better than you've gotten so far.

It's a message that millions have bought into — literally. Throngs of people in search of a new vision stormed the book-stores for *The Secret*. *The Secret* is the doctrinal creed the sec-ular espouse as they tap into the Universal spigot of wealth, health, and a life of excess.

The Secret says people get rich because they think rich. They dwell on wealth day and night. They think about all the ways in which money enhances their lives. They think about how much they love money and how much money loves them. They are the money bomb.

The Secret says this happens because of a universal law called the law of attraction. The universe brings good things into our lives because we expect nothing less. The only reason people live in poverty is because they aren't thinking positive thoughts. Negative thoughts are a barrier. Entertaining them will stop the flow of money into our lives. We need to remember that prosperity is our birthright.

The John 3:16 of the Gospel of Entitlement can be summed up as we deserve every good thing that comes our way because we, after all, made it happen by believing in it and summon-ing it to ourselves through our awesome unwavering faith in ourselves.

Hallelujah for us!

Negative thinking wreaks havoc on our lives. If we're sick we have no one to blame but ourselves. All of humanity's ills, including disease and poverty, are the result of our own negative spirits. If we aren't wealthy and healthy we have no one to blame but ourselves.

That's what the Gospel of Entitlement teaches to believers of all faith traditions and even to those who consider Jesus a cool dude and nothing more.

Dare I say this?

What a bunch of crock.

Hooey.

Bull-pukey.

You want to know the real secret?

Millions have been duped. Those who sit in the big stadium downtown listening to Preacher Smiley and those who sit on yoga mats at their home mentally flipping through the Universal Shopping Network.

They have gleaned golden nuggets from Dr. Norman Vincent Peale's controversial 1952 book — *The Power of Positive Thinking* — and repackaged it. They've made it slicker. Put it in DVD and YouTube format. They recruited a top-notch marketing team and then they took their message to the masses, who bought it, thus, making the huckster's dreams for riches come true.

The grandfather of the positive-thinking baby-boomer crowd, Dr. Peale was a motivational speaker, not a trained psychiatrist. Professionals in the field of psychiatry took issue with his cheery outlook on life. One labeled Peale's approach as "saccharine terrorism." By urging people to avoid any negative thoughts or emotions, Peale turned a blind eye to the suffering of others, thus negating any obligation to truly help them, his critics charged.

The law of attraction goes a Mother-May-I-Giant-Step

further than Dr. Peale's approach. Adherents to the universal law believe that good things come into their lives because of their own goodness. And conversely, if bad things are happening to another, it's because unfortunate souls are attracting those things to themselves — despair, suffering, depression, poverty, illness, you name it. Whether it's taught by Bible-thumping preachers or by New Age gurus with Aussie accents, the Gospel of Entitlement is, at its core, a Ponzi scheme on steroids.

It is also very uniquely American, says Michael Spencer.

"It has been the warp and woof of the American soul since the Puritans came over with their divine enlightenment and Calvinistic work ethic," Spencer says.

Spencer is a bible scholar who is best known as the blogger at InternetMonk.com, and one of Prosperity Gospel's most vocal critics.

The messages delivered by Joel Osteen and purported in *The Secret* are just different parts of the same continuum, says Spencer. "They are both speaking to the American sense of entitlement."

While the Prosperity Gospel can be found in other countries, Spencer says it takes its purest form in America.

"It is deeply wound up in who we are and far more mainstream than Joel Osteen. I grew up hearing my entire life that if you tithe, God will pay all your bills," Spencer says. "That entire thing, that absolute assumption, is a version of Prosperity Gospel thinking. All sorts of good people believe that. It's deeply embedded in us."

Is it any wonder, then, that during our nation's biggest economic crisis since the Great Depression, Joel Osteen packed Yankee Stadium with 50,000 people paying fifteen smacks a head? Spencer, who considers himself a pretty good study of

Osteen, says the media-savvy preacher started out trying to preach like his seminary-trained father but, lacking the education his father possessed, Osteen realized that method wasn't a good fit for him.

So he made what Spencer refers to as a "culturally brilliant decision" and masterfully crafted a message from the mythology that goes right back to the roots of this country. A message that promises people that if they just follow the formula, they, too, can fulfill the American dream of having the biggest house with the most cars in the neighborhood. Or as Osteen told the crowd gathered at Yankee Stadium: "As you take steps toward your destiny, God will show up. You have to put a demand on your faith. Expect to have courage you didn't have before. God will bring in the right people and the right opportunity. That's God taking your ordinary and making it extraordinary. 'No good thing will God withhold when you walk uprightly.' . . . you may not have the resources right now. That's okay. God does."[2]

Make no mistake about it, by resources, Osteen means mo' money.

We gain a certain amount of power by believing that if we act a certain way, God is going to react in the way we anticipate, Spencer says. "That gives us significance and control and an amazing outcome if we do enough of the right things."

If we have to have religion and it appears that we do, then the prosperity gospel offers us a pretty good option.

"It's a spirituality that doesn't cramp anyone's style," Spencer says.

Real problems arise, however, when such a theology is exported to lands governed by tribal rule. Spencer believes this theology reaches toxic levels when we mix this notion of earning God's favor with the indigenous tribal mentality concerning spiritual powers, and add in the ravenous hunger of other cultures for all this stuff that Americans possess.

In essence what Joel Osteen and his ilk are doing is nothing short of sheer exploitation. They've pimped out Jesus like some pale-skinned Puff Daddy. They've rolled out a life-sized cardboard cutout of a slap-happy Jesus under the glaring lights of center stage to better showcase the Rolex and diamond-encrusted bling adorning the Better Christ Now to the squealing delight of the mesmerized Home Shopping Network crowd.

"I wish he wouldn't say he was an evangelical, preaching Jesus," says Spencer. "I wish he'd say what he really is — a good motivational speaker."

If a person were to listen to the Cardboard Jesus closely enough they might hear him singing the lyrics of "Mo Money Mo Problems": "I don't know what they want from me. It's like the more money we come across, the more problems we see."

But to be fair Osteen isn't the only preacher culling promises from the generalities offered in the wisdom literature of Proverbs. He's simply the most successful at it. This "Get up, work hard, and you'll be wealthy," is preached from thousands of pulpits as a direct promise from God rather than as the principle it is intended, simply as a general rule of thumb.

The folksy Osteen comes across as harmless but the gospel he's selling isn't. The wounded in this world are dying and despairing by the thousands while prosperity preachers are offering up home-brewed remedies of Entitlement theology. These charlatans are selling salve to the sick when salvation is what people really need to fix what's ailing them.

"On what other subject was Jesus so plain?" Spencer asks. "You cannot worship God and money. God didn't leave us in the dark about that."

THE GRILL MAN

HIS GRILL IS AS BIG AS A FORD TRUCK. SERIOUSLY. HE THROWS a hog on that thing and cooks it splayed out like a meat rug, simmering. Sometimes he barbecues enough chicken to feed an entire military company. He's got a contract to do just that. Once a month he feeds soldiers returning home from deployments in Iraq and Afghanistan. Four hundred of them for two days straight.

He wasn't always a grill man. He used to work for a communications cable company, alongside his best buddies. He'd grown up an Army brat. Moving from town to town, base to base.

"I think everybody should have that experience," he said. "When you're a military kid you learn to get along with everybody. Your friends are white, black, Mexican. There's no racism. Everybody gets along."

There are definite divisions in the town where he now lives. A white side and a black side. White churches and black churches. Because it's in the South, however, people are cordial to one another. Mannerly.

The Grill Man's diner is around the corner from the District. There are over a hundred historical homes in the District. Most have white columns and leaded glass windows and porches that wrap all the way around the house like a hoop skirt fashioned from wood. The sidewalks throughout town are wide. Grandmother trees reach their limbs over the sidewalks, across the streets spreading a weave of red-and-gold in the autumn and emerald-velvet in the spring. Children ride their bikes to town or push around those two-wheeled Razor scooters. Brightly-colored helmets are the only sign that their mommas might be the least bit worried about them.

"It's a quiet town," said the Grill Man.

He leaned on his elbows, fingers folded together, across a chest-high counter. It was homemade, the counter, crafted from heart-pine and a thick layer of shellac. A dozen artificial flowers were placed neatly in a dozen vases filled with rock-salt for balance and weight on all the tables.

The Grill Man keeps his hair short, but not like a soldier, more like a deacon or politician. There's a style to it, short as it is.

He's got a round face, the face of a boy who hasn't yet lost the baby fat in his cheeks. But the Grill Man is tall and fit and could make a five-dollar suit look tailor made. He speaks with the dialect of news anchor Brian Williams, a pattern void of place or race. Another one of those traits common among Army brats.

The Grill Man takes one vacation a year — to the Super Bowl. It doesn't matter where it's at — Tampa, Miami, Phoenix — he's there.

"Uh-oh," he said. He rubbed a thick hand across the top of his head. "I was at the barbershop earlier. I just realized I left my Super Bowl hat there."

But he does not go to the Super Bowl for the football. He doesn't even follow the NFL very much.

"I go for the atmosphere," he said. "The city that hosts the Super Bowl puts on a lot of free stuff. Concerts of Rhythm and Blues, Jazz, Gospel. I get to hear a lot of different kinds of music. People think the Super Bowl is just a one-day event but it's a week long. I really enjoy it."

At forty-two, the Grill Man has never been married.

"The opportunity never presented itself," he said, then turned and strode into the kitchen, laughing. Later, he admitted that he has three different daughters by three different women.

"It ain't right but that was before I was saved," he said. "I try to do right by them. I take care of them. I provide for them financially and try to teach them godly ways."

It was in part that financial obligation to his daughters that led the Grill Man to his calling.

"I started taking up orders," he said.

That's rural town's terminology for being a runner. He'd go around to local businesses, take their lunch orders — always the same, chicken or pork barbecue. Then he'd get the orders from a diner and deliver them back to the businesses.

For his own lunch, he'd usually get a barbecue turkey sandwich from Mr. Ernest.

Barbecue turkey?

"That's what everybody says — at first," he said. The Grill Man walked to the kitchen, put some shredded turkey into a plastic cup, and stuck a plastic fork into it. "Try this."

Then he went on with his story.

"Mr. Ernest made it in his home. He told me to try it one day. I liked it. He'd leave my lunch in a sack on my grandmother's doorstep."

Eventually, Mr. Ernest taught the Grill Man how to make his own turkey barbecue. And not long after that Mr. James, another fellow, showed the Grill Man how to cook a hog on the grill.

"Mr. James turned me loose one day to cook for a funeral and everybody said it was good," he recalled.

The Grill Man continued taking up orders for folks, and counting the money that came in with large groups, and pretty soon, he realized there was good money to be made in the feeding business.

"Nobody was doing chipped barbecue in Carolina," he said.

The Grill Man handed a customer a brown sack, top folded down. Six-year-old Preston stood on his tip-toes and pushed his buck-fifty across the counter and took his hot dog — ketchup only — home.

"See ya later," Preston said, waving goodbye.

"Later," the Grill Man replied.

Preston is only one of dozens of faithful customers that the Grill Man serves each day. Most come for the turkey barbecue. He fills orders for turkey barbecue from as far away as Detroit and Dallas.

"Everybody got on this health kick," the Grill Man explained.

He starts his grilling every morning between two and three a.m., and works the diner until closing — usually about seven p.m. The menu sides include boiled potatoes or cabbage, mac-and-cheese, green beans.

The Grill Man believes that one day he'll be selling turkey barbecue all around the world.

"I've been blessed with this talent and I've got the favor of God on my life right now. Everything I touch turns out good."

He's not just talking turkey. He really believes that God has blessed him, will continue to bless him, and will one day bless him in even bigger ways, with riches untold.

It was prayer that led him to the business to start with, he explained. He'd come to the diner to fix an air conditioner, another one of those odd jobs he'd do to pick up extra cash.

"I didn't have any money," he said. "None in the bank, none nowhere, and I had bad credit."

That morning, before he set out, he'd prayed for God to give him a place to start his own business. The woman who owned the diner at the time had uttered a prayer herself that morning — she'd prayed for somebody to buy her business.

Citing Matthew 18:20 — "Wherever two or more are gathered together in my name, I am there in the midst of them" — the Grill Man pointed to their individual prayers as proof that God was leading him. That the previous diner owner worked a deal with him, despite his lack of funds and bad credit, was only further affirmation that he was doing the thing he was designed to do.

"All I had was God's favor," he said.

Two years have passed since the Grill Man first walked into the diner to fix an air conditioner. Despite the tight economy, business is going well. People are still eating. He's not the least bit surprised at his success.

"The way God is leading me I don't think I can fail. That's not arrogance, that's just inner confidence."

It's a confidence that has its roots in a formulaic theology. He believes that a person can earn the favor of God.

"There are certain principles you've got to follow. You've got to apply the Word of God to your life. I tithe faithfully because tithing is my obligation but also because God will reward me for it."

But then the Grill Man backs off his own prosperity teaching for a moment and offers a word of caution — rewards won't always come in a monetary fashion. God likes to mix it up, keep a fellow on his toes.

"Sometimes it's encouragement. Sometimes encouragement may be more important than money," he explained. "I don't think God's favor is all about finances, but I don't exclude finances, either."

Obtaining such favor is a spiritual chess game of sorts, where position is everything.

"I am trying to position myself so that when the floodgates open, I'm ready," the Grill Man said.

And what if true lovers of turkey barbecue never grow beyond the confines of downtown's Historic District? What does that mean for the Grill Man?

"It won't be God's fault," he said. "It'll be because of something I'm doing wrong. Some principle I'm ignoring."

He's not worried about that, though. The Grill Man is a believer, and the thing he believes in is a God who is going to give him the desires of his heart.

"I've got something big inside of me trying to get out. I'm hungry and satisfied at the same time."

It might be difficult to crawl out of bed before three a.m. and fire up the grill every morning, but with that gnawing hunger inside the Grill Man's belly, he greets each day with great expectations.

"I would never limit God to just a double-wide."

He means it. The Grill Man is expecting bigger and better than that.

THE GIVER

S HE MOVES GENTLY THROUGH THE WORLD, CAREFUL TO NOT take up too much space or be a burden to anyone. Whenever there's a crowd 'round, be it a family gathering or strangers not yet dear friends, she is the one who wipes the counters clean and puts on another pot of coffee for everyone to enjoy.

Nearly every other day the Giver sits at the dining room table with a stack of cards and handwrites birthday and anniversary wishes. She sends out twenty-five to thirty such personal greetings each month, and many more than that during the months of August and September. Blame it on those long, dark nights of January.

Sending a card for a birthday or anniversary may not seem like much of a ministry, but it's the one the Giver could handle with ease after a debilitating lung disorder left her short of breath and even shorter of physical energy. Kids now grown know that when other family and friends forget, they can always count on their beloved adopted aunt to remember their birthdays.

She was born to nurture the multitudes, though she's never had any children of her own. That uterus had given her fits since she was a teenage girl and a blood vessel ruptured. Doctors finally removed the uterus decades later, after it got wrapped around itself and nearly killed her.

Even then, after she'd been deprived of the ability to ever bear one single solitary child to cherish, she did not complain about how unfairly life has treated her. The Giver never thinks about what life has taken from her. She only thinks about all that God has given her and all the ways in which she can show her gratitude.

She was raised up the oldest of four children, the family's only girl. She thinks that's where she first learned to not be a burden to anyone. She remembers how busy her mama was with all those boys to see about. So she crafted herself into a contented soul. A person determined not to be a bother to her mama or anyone else.

The Giver was one of the brightest females in a high school that numbered in the thousands. She graduated with that school's highest honors. She could have done anything — been a bank executive or big-shot engineer, if that had been her choice, but it wasn't. She became a teacher. A home economics teacher. They don't even give out degrees in that anymore, do they?

Becoming a teacher was a natural choice, she says. Her mother and father were both educators. Still, she never dreamed that she'd spend thirty years teaching middle-schoolers how to thread a sewing machine or how to preheat an oven. She expected, instead, that she would marry and have a family of her own.

"I assumed I would grow up, get married, and someone would help provide for me," she says. "But I learned right quick that just getting a paycheck didn't mean having your needs met, so I learned to look to God. Ultimately, he is the one who meets my needs."

She never felt a specific call to singleness; though, she says, if she had been raised up Catholic, she probably would have been a nun. The Giver would likely be equally as happy as a long-haul truck driver or a toll-booth attendant. She embodies contentment.

It's a choice, she says, this ability to take whatever comes or doesn't come her way.

"Being married is just something that never happened. I didn't consciously turn away from it. It just never came," she says. "But it's like everything else. It's a choice to be content. I'm single today but I don't know what tomorrow might hold. I trust that nobody wants better for me than what God does."

Most people who talk about God wanting better for them talk about it in terms of a better job and a bigger home. When they pray for God to increase their territory, they really are asking for God to double their stock portfolio. But when the Giver talks about how God wants better for her, she's talking about God's heart toward her.

For nearly thirty years now, the Giver has lived in a 550-square-foot garage apartment. It sits up high among the pine trees. Her closest neighbors are the redbirds, the woodpeckers, and the squirrels. She pays $145 a month for the one-bedroom abode.

She could afford more, but she's never seen the sense of that.

"Not to say I wouldn't love to have more space, just one more room maybe to keep things in, to have projects in. But I ask myself, do I want to spend $400 or $600 more a month just to have more room? It's not worth it to me, given the other things I'd have to give up, so I stay where I'm at."

You might be wondering if the Giver has a shoe obsession that requires most of her discretionary funds.

It's true, she does own a pair of name-brand tennis shoes that cost her as much as one-month's rent, but as she'll explain to anyone who notices, her doctor encouraged her to buy them. They help with a toe-joint problem.

No one who has ever met her would accuse the fifty-four-year-old Giver of being a fashionista. She dresses the same as she lives — simply and comfortably. Her hair, graying now, is cut primly. Her skin, rarely exposed to the Georgia sun, is flawless, free of freckles or wrinkles.

Giving, she says, is her spiritual gift.

"When I see a situation, I think, what can I give to help make that person's situation better? In my case it might be giving $50 or $100 or whatever. I think that's my motivational gift that God has given me to minister to his body."

She's the woman who puts $20 in the hands of another and says, "Here's you some coke money." That's what her grand-daddy used to call it — coke money. Just a little something extra to brighten a person's day. Only in the days her granddaddy gave out coke money, 25 cents would buy a person soda and a pack of crackers. That $20 won't even buy a kid a tank of gas these days. But it is the Giver's way of saying to another, "You matter to me."

The couch in her tree-house apartment is the same one she moved in with. Only the bed is new, a gift to herself upon her retirement from teaching. Two window units, one in the dining room and the other in the bedroom, help keep the apartment cool in those sticky-hot Georgia summers. Those units are a welcome relief. She lived there a couple of years without air conditioning of any sort.

She's not frugal so that she can hoard her money. She's frugal because it makes her happy to help out others. That's the thing about being a giver, your joy comes from being able to do for others.

"So often I wish I could give more," she says. "I can't help everybody but I can do what God enables me to do with my resources. I try not to be overwhelmed by the needs of others but to discern what I can do and then do it. That's the joy and the contentment. Everything I have comes from God and is God's. He's enabled me to work for it, and ultimately he has provided it."

You won't find her name on the list of big donors at any of the charitable organizations around town. There are no wings at the local hospital or the local university named for her or her loved ones. There's a quiet to her giving that only those who love her best recognize.

"I'll give you an example," she says. "Back when the nieces and nephew were little, I knew it was expensive for their mamas and daddies to get those kids ready for the school year. So I decided that I would buy the kids new underwear for school every year. It was a very little thing, but it was something the families didn't have to budget for. I did that until the kids got out of college. I enjoyed doing that every year. It made me feel like I was getting ready to go back to school."

Her giving goes beyond her tithing, which she is always faithful to fulfill. There are missions here and abroad. And the Valley Rescue, which serves critters in need. Animals instinctively take to her. Stray cats wait outside her door in the winter because they know she'll invite them in to sit a spell. Dogs whose owners talk sternly to them will take refuge at her feet, like a child hiding behind his mama's apron. She speaks to them in whispers of encouragement.

The Giver is not prone to flashes of anger. When she's frustrated, she might go so far as to call a person a knucklehead. Her only cuss words are spelled out, rather than spoken aloud, thus deflating their impact. It's just one other aspect to her moving gently through the world.

She's never demanded anything of God, not even his attention. Trusting him was something she learned to do.

"There was never this moment of grand revelation," she says. "I think it all came about as a result of growing up in the church and learning and growing in faith and experiencing it for myself. When you see God meet a need, it grows your faith and it's easier to trust God the next time a need comes up."

She has never held to the notion that God, or anybody else for that matter, owed her anything.

"I've always felt that he's promised to meet my needs, but I never thought he was going to make me rich," she says. "I never thought, I'll give God 20 percent so he'll give me 60 percent. To me that kind of thinking negates the motivation for giving to begin with. How I'm blessed beyond my needs is totally up to God and not based upon what I've given."

In other words, she doesn't buy into that whole equation of "giving for getting's" sake. She's not giving to test God, to see if he really will open up the storehouse of heaven for her. She's not giving beyond her measure so that one day she'll have a McMansion at the end of Living Good Lane.

She gives solely for the pleasure of giving.

"The thing about giving being your gifting is that the joy is in the giving. It's its own reward. You've been able to see a need and to be in a position to help."

When you live your life the way the Giver does, consumerism holds no sway over you and your emotions.

"It doesn't take a lot for me to be happy. I've always been that way. I know society wants to make me feel like I don't measure up. That I don't have enough. But I've got a good dose of common sense and I know that's not so. That's not what life is all about."

The Giver has never been found lacking.

"I've been blessed from the standpoint of never having any catastrophic need."

She does not live in debt of any sort and considers herself fortunate to have avoided what has become a trap for so many others.

"I realized early on that debt was not a way to live. Sometimes you can't help it but I don't want to be in debt for anything. I may not be rich by a lot of people's standards. I realize it's considered un-American not to be seduced by sex or money. But I have what I need. There is nothing I have a great desire for."

It disturbs her the way too many folks get caught up in chasing after the wrong things. And it downright angers her the way so many are willing to cheat others for selfish gain.

"It's very distressing to me that somebody can take from people who have worked hard for their money. That they take advantage of them and have literally stolen from them. I have nothing against people who prosper through hard work. I don't begrudge them, but if you are going to steal from others to get ahead, I don't get that one bit. How can you enjoy something you've stolen from others?"

That's a question Bernie Madoff will have plenty of time to ponder as he sits in that jail cell for the rest of his borne days, and if he doesn't come up with a better answer before this life is over, maybe on into his eternity.

The Giver will likely never live high on the hog but don't pity her. She's perfectly content.

"I realize that life is more than our possessions. When it is all said and done, that's not what matters. I'm not going to lay dying, thinking, I wish I had one more day to shop or I wish I owned one more thing. That's not why I live. That's not why I get up in the morning. I get a lot of pleasure out of what I'm able to do and give to others, not what I do for myself."

For the Giver, living the good life can be boiled down to living a life doing good.

THE MISSIONARY

S HE DIED IN HIS ARMS. WHENEVER HE TURNS ON THE television and hears another slick-haired preacher pontificating about wealth, the Missionary thinks of that day he carried the nine-year-old from her jungle home to the airstrip. Internal parasites had infested her tiny brown body and were eating her up from the inside out.

He prayed as he carried her. Prayed he could get her to the plane in time. Prayed the plane would get her to the hospital in Quito in time, but she died in his arms before he reached that plane.

It was an antibiotic, not a miracle, she needed. The medicine that could have healed her would have cost a few pennies a dose. He thinks of that as he scans the television screen.

"The first thing I do when I see those preachers is look at their hands to see how many diamond rings they're wearing," he says. "When I see them in their glass palaces or big stadiums, I think of her. That money should be put to good use helping little girls like the one I carried to the airstrip. That's where all that money should be going."

He stops himself abruptly.

The mighty heart behind his barrel chest has weakened, the

result of congestive heart disease and the burden of grief he's carried for a native child for forty years now. He exhales, purposely deflating the frustration that can so easily turn to anger.

"I can't go down that road," he says. Minutes later he's drawn back in, like a dog circling a campfire staring into the dangerous flames. "All she needed was some medication."

It wasn't God who failed that little girl. We did. Those of us who spend our money mindlessly, selfishly, instead of purposefully helping dying children the world over.

"We have such a small worldview and such an inflated view of who we really are," says the Missionary.

We distort John 10:10 and Jeremiah 29:11. The Missionary says the verses that talk about abundant life and God's desire to prosper us have nothing to do with money.

"We get things confused," he says. "We only think of wealth in monetary terms. It's not about being rich, it's about having a rich way of life."

The Missionary has never had much money. In four decades, the highest paying job he secured as a minister earned him a whopping $1100 a month. That's a far cry below the kind of salary he could have made, if only.

★

He grew up in Chief Joseph country, where God tucked away a stash of rough-cut mountains, several crystal glacier lakes, and acres of emerald meadows. These were the treasures the Missionary knew back when he was nothing more than the Farmer's crippled boy.

"Back in those days men counted their wealth in the sons they had. Sons were your work force. My brothers were all pretty sound, and then there was me. In my dad's words, he had this 'damn cripple boy.'"

It made him feel gosh-awful bad to hear his father talk about him that a'way. It wasn't like it was his fault he was a cripple. He'd been born perfectly healthy and stayed that way till somebody, likely somebody from outside the county, brought in that paralyzing polio virus. Nearly killed him too, but even as a three-year-old, the boy possessed a defying willfulness.

The youth didn't have any notion what a life with money looked like until he took his first trip to Portland when he was ten.

"I couldn't believe it. Man, everybody was running around in cars, in trucks, and in buses. There were huge stores downtown where a person could buy anything they wanted. I must have looked like one of those jungle tribal people wandering around Quito for the first time. It was all just so mind-staggering to me."

But the boy hadn't come to Portland to shop. He'd come to have surgery. He didn't have a dime in his lint-filled pocket, but those kindly Shriners had seen to all his needs. It wasn't going to cost his daddy one Lincoln penny, which was a good thing considering if it had, he'd still be back on the farm.

They didn't have electricity or running water or indoor plumbing on the farm, but it never occurred to the boy that his family was poor. Far as he was concerned, except for that bum leg of his, he was like every other kid struggling to learn reading and sums in that two-room schoolhouse they attended.

"I didn't know we were poor until sometime in the 1940s when the government came out with its standard of living numbers and told us we were," he says, laughing.

Despite his affliction, he made out pretty good. Much better than his daddy figured he would, given that dragging leg of his. At age twenty-five he'd worked his way up to being the millwright at the local sawmill. It was one of the best jobs in the lumber business. He was making $4 an hour, over twice what the other boys working the green chain or planer were drawing down.

It wasn't what he wanted to be doing, though. What he wanted was to be a landowner like his daddy. So every paycheck his bride was putting money aside, storing for the day when they would buy a farm of their own. A place with cattle and horses and maybe some sheep, if he wanted.

He wishes still that he could have bought his daddy's farm. The homeplace sat on 680 acres, and his father had an additional 2300 acres that they ran the livestock on during the summer. Flooding was the only form of irrigation they had back then. It took a lot of land to make farming profitable. There just wasn't enough land to divvy up between five kids and have any of them make a living off it.

"You could only irrigate where the water would naturally flow. I carried a shovel around, trying to walk the water around the fields," he says.

★

The Missionary might have been a tall man had the polio not robbed him of a couple inches. He has his boots custom-made, designed with a lift to help keep his back and hips in alignment. He has the angular face of a Marine Sergeant and the stout shoulders of one too. His arms are still strong enough to wrestle cattle. It's likely he would have had plenty of cattle, too, on that farm he hoped to call his own one day, had it not been for God calling him out to the mission field. Most everybody thought he'd taken leave of his senses when he announced that he was leaving the mill job and was going to prepare for work in missions.

Good Lord. What was he thinking?

Prior to that he'd been, in his own words, "an ornery, mean rounder from the backwoods of Northeastern Oregon."

It was easy to figure out why.

"My father's bitterness had splashed over into my life too many times. I was full of hate and anger."

But once he decided to take God at his word, he began to change from the inside out.

"Tom Fair, an old evangelist, was holding meetings in town. He'd been a knot-head of a wild guy with an alcohol problem like I was."

When the evangelist extended an altar call, the Missionary responded. By the time he'd concentrated his life to the Lord for good, he was married and had two children.

It was on one Easter morning while reading through Matthew 28:18–20, the Great Commission verses instructing believers to go and make disciples of all men, that the Missionary first felt a stirring. He conferred with his pastor, who encouraged him to seek God.

"Have you asked him what he wants you to do with your life?" the pastor asked.

Nope. The Missionary reckoned he had never thought to do that. So he and the missus began to pray about the matter, one thing led to another, and pretty soon they were packing up the house and moving to Portland so he could go to Bible college for a couple of years and they could prepare for a life in missions.

It wasn't as simple as all that, that's just the simplest way to explain the convoluted path that led the rounder from Eastern Oregon to the jungles of Ecuador.

"The thing that really made me take stock of what we were about to do was when some of the Christian fellows I respected came to me and asked if I realized what I was doing and had I considered my family's security and welfare?" the Missionary says.

The decision to go to the field left more than just his Christian buddies shaking their befuddled heads. His father was adamantly opposed to the decision. The Farmer went to an attorney to try and stop the Missionary from taking his precious grandchildren off to the jungle wilds around all those dangerous animals and naked people. The attorney advised the Farmer that there was little he could do to stop a man with a mission.

If that wasn't bad enough, the Missionary got a call from his own son's teacher one day. The third-grader had written a letter in class expressing his frustration over the move. He said he wished he were dead. That's how badly the little boy didn't want to leave behind all things familiar.

"All of this worked into the equation, it was all the stuff we were struggling with in our own minds at the time," he says. "It was very tough. The Enemy kept throwing things up that made us blink twice."

He would never have gone on the mission field if his wife hadn't also felt called to go. Still, it was harder on her in many ways.

"I don't want to make it sound like it was an easy step, it was very difficult. My wife is a nester and she liked having the security of home," he says.

The couple kept a drawing of the dream home they hoped to build one day hanging in their bedroom. While he was attending Bible College, he had continued to work in a mill at the shipyards in Vancouver, Washington. When his boss heard that he was considering leaving for the mission field he called a meeting. The boss told the Missionary that he didn't want him to leave, that he needed him, that he had hoped to move him into management soon.

"They were a start-up company that in three-and-half years had gone to making over $800,000 gross," the Missionary says. "They considered me more than just a flunky. They thought of me as someone who added value to their organization. They wanted to keep me around."

His boss told him that if he would stay, they would build him that dream home. The Missionary was flattered but he was not dissuaded.

"By that time we were pretty well-pointed in the direction God wanted us to go. I told him I was sorry but that I was sure that this is where God wanted us."

One way he knew was that it hadn't taken them any time at all to raise the support they'd need. Most of the funds came from people with very little money. Rural folks, many who'd never even made the day's drive across the state to see the Pacific Ocean pounding Oregon's craggy shores, but who understood that when God calls a fella he'd better go, even it that means going to some faraway land filled with venomous snakes and bright-butt monkeys.

"I still can't believe how quickly it all came together. I think the Lord did all that quickly before we could change our minds."

★

His father had every right to be worried. The Missionary and his family were sent to serve the Auca people, one of the seven tribes they served in Ecuador. The indigenous tribe appeared on the international scene in January, 1956 when it was discovered that five young men, missionaries all, had been slaughtered by local tribesmen.

Those men — Jim Elliot, Ed McCully, Roger Youderian, Pete Fleming, and Nate Saint — left behind wives and young children. Two women, Elizabeth Elliot, wife of Jim, and Rachel Saint, sister to Nate, remained in the field and continued the work they had begun. The Missionary and his family joined in that effort.

There was Bible teaching to be sure, but there were also lessons about crops, about animals, about machinery. And in the 1960s when the polio epidemic swept through the camp, leaving a dozen or so lame, the Missionary and his wife set up a physical therapy hut in Limoncocha.

"We were able to rehab all but two of them," the Missionary says.

Using banana stalks and papayas for weights (known as *functional substitutes* to those in the field), the Missionary taught the afflicted the dozens and dozens of exercises he had been taught as a young boy at Portland's Shriners' Hospital. Day after hot day, for six agonizing weeks, they would gather in that hut and groan through the repetitive muscle-strengthening routines.

"God used my own experience with polio in such a marvelous way. That I was able to work with them in that way went a long ways toward winning their confidence and, ultimately, in sharing the gospel."

And the little boy who had written that note to his third-grade teacher, saying he'd rather die than head to the jungle? He flourished there.

"He helped with the livestock and became my chief translator," the Missionary says. "He picked up the language so fast that he tagged along with me, to help translate for me."

The boy told his mother, "Do you know the greatest thing about being out here? We have Dad for breakfast, we have Dad for lunch, and we have Dad for dinner."

There was even another son born in-country. It's likely the Missionary and his wife would be there yet had it not been for the lung infection that ailed him. Doctors forbid him from returning to a humid climate. He would need arid air from then on out.

★

The Missionary does not long for the dream home he could never afford. He has no regrets about walking away from the promise of a corporate job and all the benefits that would have entailed. The opportunity to serve others is all that's ever really mattered to him.

He counts his riches in the letters stacked on his desk. Many of which contain the stories of the work that continues in the land of venomous snakes and bright-butt monkeys. The tribal people are no longer called the Aucas, a pejorative term that meant *savage*. Now they are known as the Waodani, *the People*, and many are known as a *God Follower*.

If you speak to him of what prosperity means, he will quote to you from Psalm 18:2: "The Lord is my rock, my fortress and my deliverer. My God is my rock, in whom I take refuge. He is my shield and the horn of my salvation, my stronghold."

"That to me is the greatest picture of God's provision anywhere," he says.

Anyone who stands behind a pulpit or before a television audience and proclaims a Genie-in-a-Jug-Jesus is just plain wrong.

"How many of those believers would stand up for their faith if their house was being burned or their family was being beaten? What would their testimony be then?" the Missionary asks.

More importantly, what words would they have uttered if they had been the ones carrying the fever-ravaged girl to the plane that day? Would they have inquired of her, "Do you want to be well or do you want to continue lying around feeling sorry for yourself?" Or would they have admonished her, "You can think yourself to the perfect state of health"?

What good, pray tell, is their Genie-in-a-Jug-Jesus when children lay dying?

THE EMPLOYEE

S HE DOESN'T LOOK AT HER 401(K) STATEMENT ANYMORE. "I haven't looked because I don't want to get upset," says the Employee. "A couple of years ago our stock was trading at $70 and $80 a share. Yesterday people were excited because it went up from 34 cents a share to $1 a share."

She's worked for the company for a very long time, ever since way back when, long before it was associated with American International Group (AIG). Back when it was just a well-respected local company built from the ground up by a fellow who lived in the community. There's something to be said for that.

When you run a company that's tied to a community you feel a certain sense of obligation to do right by your neighbors. You have to look these people in the eye at the grocery store and at ballgames and at church. There's a certain accountability that was lost when the company was taken over by AIG.

The takeover took place very quickly. Employees who had been with the company for decades heard the rumors of a takeover. "People were predicting that we were going to be acquired. We knew somebody was probably going to buy us," she says. They just weren't exactly sure who that somebody would be. When it actually happened, nobody knew what to expect.

"Because we had always been the company that was acquiring other companies."

They hoped it might mean better benefits, better pay, but it didn't work out that way. Talk about your irony of ironies. You could almost feel the reverberations of foreboding things to come shake the glass walls of the corporation. The first thing AIG did was come in with a new rulebook. No more local vendors. They had to use pre-approved vendors.

"AIG used its size to get volume discounts."

Great idea, except when that meant dealing with vendors in a city three hours away, instead of the local fellows just up the street. The Employee remembers talking with an AIG representative from New York City.

"I wanted to tell her to get her atlas out and take a look at her geography," the Employee recalls. "They didn't understand what kind of problems it can cause to work with a vendor three hours away. It made it so much harder to do business. We had to do a lot of hollering and swinging of the elbows before they understood. For the most part AIG does not bend. AIG does not flex. You play by their rules or you just don't play, and that's just the way it is."

If you really want to try and understand what happens when a local company is acquired by a firm like AIG, imagine it in terms of a house, says the Employee. If you have a 1,300-square-foot home that needs to be moved, it might take some work, but you could move it, cinder-block foundation and all. You can't do that with a skyscraper. The bigger the company, the bigger problems it poses, and as everyone who hasn't been in a coma these past few years knows, AIG is the mother of all this nation's financial problems as of late.

The Employee didn't know a thing about those problems

until she walked into her glass office on September 15, 2008. As far as she knows, none of the mucky-mucks she works with knew anything either.

"Even those people who were friends with the VP here didn't know a thing about it. They honestly didn't know," she says. "The upper management here is just as furious with AIG as the little folks like me. Our company had been managed very well and had been very profitable over the years. To see all this happen, to see all the work you've done over the years brought down, it's sad. It makes the people here angry. Very angry."

The news that the company was really in trouble had actually made headlines the day before when the *New York Times* reported that Governor David Paterson was going to allow AIG to lend itself $20 billion to stave off potentially life-threatening credit downgrades. The company's shares had fallen 60 percent that week. The governor stated that despite the measure being taken, AIG was "financially sound."[1]

Yeah, right, and Elvis really is holed up in Vegas awaiting the second coming of Jesus.

The Employee could barely comprehend what she was hearing.

"Everybody's immediate reaction around here was, 'Oh my gosh, we are going to lose our jobs. We are going to lose our 401(k)s.'"

She locked herself into her glass shelter and sat frozen in fear. Her first thoughts weren't about her job as she knew it, but about her world as she knew it.

"What struck me that day was the realization that if a company the size of AIG could be brought to its knees, then the entire world was in trouble financially. It was a lot more serious than just us losing our jobs."

If AIG and its employees were to adopt a theme song, it might be Johnny Cash's tune, "Ring of Fire": "I fell into a burning ring of fire. I went down, down, down and the flames went higher."

It's since become apparent that New York Governor Paterson was either lying when he said the company was financially sound or sorely misinformed. The company continued to spiral headlong into controversy. Because of AIG's far-reaching sticky fingers, government officials have continued to shore up the company with bailout funds, a whopping $180 billion and counting, even as the company continues to report losses — $99 billion in 2008.[2]

What really tweaked off the masses, however, wasn't just putting a badly managed company on the public dole at taxpayers' expense, but the sheer recklessness that was part of the company's culture. An AIG subsidiary racked up a bill reaching nearly $444,000 for an executive retreat taken at the luxurious St. Regis Spa in Southern California just days after the feds granted the company an $85 billion credit line. Additionally, AIG reportedly had agreed to pay several former employees inexplicable salaries, some amounting to $1 million a month, all with public funds.[3]

On and on it goes. As the list of misconduct, mismanagement, and outright wrongdoing by AIG executives grew, the blogosphere lit up as an enraged public fought back. They assigned new definition to the company's acronym: Appalling Illustrations of Greed. Or Arrogance, Incompetence, and Greed.

The public's anger spilled over and they began to rage against anyone associated with AIG. At church people would approach the Employee and ask, "So tell me about your spa day." They would always follow it with a chuckle.

Maybe such remarks wouldn't carry such a sting had it not been for the stress of working every day for the most vilified company in America.

"We keep the security gate manned. They stop each employee now. We were told to take our ID badges off whenever we leave the building for lunch for our own protection. We are having security threats, death threats against our employees here. It is sad. Just so sad."

Believe it or not, there was a time when the Employee took pride in the job she did.

"One reason I enjoyed my job was because I was proud to work for a company that had a long and illustrious history in this community, and now to be associated with a company posting some of the biggest losses in America, it is very sad."

She's not one prone to tears. She holds her water pretty well. Still there was that day her grown son walked into the kitchen and put his arm around her shoulder and said, "It's going to be alright, Mom, but you better get your résumé ready."

She stumbles over the recollection of that moment, and swallows back a sob. The death threats unnerve her. On one hand she understands the public's disgust.

"I'm not even sure the government should have bailed AIG out, but this company is made up of so many people whose lives are tremendously impacted who don't deserve the shame of all this."

Innocent, hard-working people like her. People who've gotten up at daybreak for the past twenty, thirty, or forty years and gone to work and did the job that was required of them.

"We are just the lower rank and file. We had nothing to do with any of this. We never know if we're going to come to work one day and find the gates locked or what."

The Employee is just as angry as any taxpayer over the misconduct of AIG's management, but she says, "I don't have anyone to direct my anger to. The people responsible are so far removed from me, they are faceless. It's hard to be angry at people you don't know."

So she thinks about the people she does know and how their lives are being affected.

"I get emotional thinking about all those people. One of the ladies I work with has been with the company fifty years. She never married. She doesn't have any children. She has no one to fall back on. No one to take care of her. This company has been her whole life."

It's unfair to the employees who do their jobs faithfully, but that's what happens when greed infiltrates a culture and a company. The Employee has had her own struggles with wanting more than she's got.

"When our son was little my husband and I used to look through the home plan books and talk about the day we'd build our dream home. We both worked hard, hoping for the day that big raise came and we could afford that house."

But that raise never was big enough to build the home they dreamed of.

"It was really hard to deal with, this realization that I wasn't going to get everything I wanted out of life."

It's such a hard reality, some people never face up to it.

"Americans think they are entitled. They think, why not have what I want? Why not take out a loan and buy this $400,000 home although I only make $45,000 a year? We live in excess."

The Employee and her husband chose a more frugal route.

"We've been tempted to live beyond our means but we just felt it was wrong. You can't flourish spiritually when you are in slavery to things you own. You get overextended and it starts to control your life."

If a company like AIG gets overextended, it can control the national budget. The Employee is stumped by the spiritual lessons to be found in government bailouts.

"Gosh, I don't even know what the message of Christ would be in all of this," she says.

She ponders the matter some, then says, "I don't know how to answer that other than to say part of the problem is that we haven't had our eyes on God. It's not the government's job to take care of us, or any company. It's God's job. We need to turn to him more than ever. It's God we need to turn to because God says that even in difficult times, he's never going to leave us."

Whether you're solvent or not, that's a promise you can bank on — God is never going to lock the gates on you.

THE REDHEAD

T HE REDHEAD WAS MURDERED IN MY DREAM. IT WAS THE summer of 1998. I'd woken short of breath, heart pounding that Sunday morning. Turning to my husband, I shook him awake.

"I've had an awful dream," I said. "Something is terribly wrong with the Redhead. She's in some sort of danger."

The Redhead is one of my dearest friends. We attended the same college and married our husbands the same year. I was in her wedding. She was in mine. We each had four children. My youngest bears her name.

I told my husband about the dream without telling him what happened in the dream. No details.

"I should call Ed, warn him that his wife is in danger," I said. "Tell him to lay hands on her and pray for her."

"So call," my sleepy-eyed husband said.

"I can't," I cried.

"Why not?"

"He's an engineer," I said. "He'll think I'm nuts."

"You are nuts," my husband said, kissing my forehead.

I woke our four kids, fed them breakfast, and yelled for them to hurry up and get dressed for church. But the vivid images of the Redhead's husband searching room-to-room for his wife haunted me.

I picked up the phone and dialed the number to the sunny home on Thornton Lake. I hoped the Redhead wouldn't answer, but I knew she would. She always did.

"Good morning," I said. "Is Ed home? May I speak with him?"

If she thought it odd, and I knew she must, she didn't say. The Redhead called for her husband.

"I don't know how to explain this and I can't really," I said. "But your wife is in danger. You and the kids need to lay hands on her and pray for her."

"Okay," he said. "Thanks for calling."

Then that man, that obedient man who has loved the Redhead dearly for three decades and longer, gathered their four children around their mother and he prayed for her.

Three weeks later, she called me. They'd taken a trip to the family's summer home at the Oregon coast. She'd been in the shower when she ran her hand over her breast and discovered it.

It wasn't a pea-sized lump between soft tissues. It was stubborn and the size of a golf ball. It was a virulent, aggressive mass of cells on an angry rampage.

It was breast cancer.

They told her that after her biopsy, but she knew it before then, knew it as well as she knew her own name.

The Redhead was in the changing room at the Women's Imaging Center, clothed in a lovely calico backless gown, when she heard the click-click of the technician's heels coming down the hallway.

"I instinctively knew at that moment that the lump was cancerous," the Redhead recalls. She fought an urge to flee out the back door. Had she not been in that backless gown she might not have resisted the urge.

As the technician wheeled her toward the biopsy room, the Redhead prayed: "God, I cannot do this. Matter of fact, I won't do it! So you will have to do it for me. If you are in it God, I know there will be an eternal purpose and there has to be something of greater importance than me in all of this. So you're on God. It's all up to you to see me through this because I'm not doing it."

That was a start of a pattern for her. She turned anxiety into a tool that she could wield. Like a hunter learning to use a bow, it took time for her to figure out how to hit her target, but she's had a great deal of practice.

"I use the pain, fear, and uncertainty as a trigger to practice the presence of God. They remind me to praise God rather than to focus on that which could overtake me easily and negatively."

This is not the power of positive-thinking. It is the power of praise practiced.

"It is not automatic," the Redhead says. "It is a choice every single time."

Her fears are real. Her praise is deliberate.

"When my heart, mind, and lips are exclaiming God's character, praising him for who he is, my heart fills with gratitude and there is no room for anything like fear or self-pity."

But there has been plenty of reason to be fearful, full of self-pity, had that been her choice. First, there was surgery, followed by chemotherapy. Afterwards, she lost her trademark curly red hair. Her own daughter, the last of her four children, started kindergarten that year. Would the Daughter ever remember having a mother free from cancer?

Like most do, the Redhead sought favor from God. But the

favor she sought didn't have anything to do with money — it was about something much more precious. She asked God to let her keep a bright countenance.

"So that people don't feel sadness or pity for me," she prayed. "Rather, fill me with yourself so that your character, hope, and joy shine through and draw others to yourself. Help me to embrace you fully and use the cancer as a catalyst for a greater purpose than myself."

The goal was clear. If cancer was going to invade her life, she wanted to use it as a tool for bringing honor and glory to God. That was the only way the journey would be of any value, she says.

To the casual passerby, the Redhead appears to have a storybook life. There's the home with the glass-paned windows on the lake edged in lily-pads. The house is surrounded by flowers, bushes of yellow mums in the fall and pots of bright red geraniums all summer long.

There are framed snapshots of the blond-headed children, three boys and one girl, grown now, on the polished wood buffet. There's even a painting of the Redhead as a child, grasping a tin watering pot as she sprinkles the flowers in her own mother's garden.

There's a rope swing in the big tree out front and a gingerbread-laced dollhouse that looks like something Martha Stewart might have designed. This is the house where all the cousins came every summer for an entire week of "Cousin Camp."

The Redhead planned it all out in advance. The mornings at Vacation Bible School, the afternoons of arts-and-crafts or lazy canoe trips around the lake. A competitive swimmer in high school, the Redhead never lost her love of the water. She passed that love on to her own children.

She's fond of saying that she wears rose-colored glasses. The

Redhead appreciates all things beautiful, whether it's the fine china she bought while visiting her sister in London or a plate of freshly baked cookies that she's covered with Saran Wrap and tied off with a golden bow. Every gift she's ever given has been lavishly adorned.

She takes to heart the admonishment of Philippians 4:8: "Finally, brothers, whatever is true, whatever is honorable, whatever is fair, whatever is pure, whatever is acceptable, whatever is commendable, if there is anything of excellence and if there is anything praiseworthy — keep thinking about these things."

If anyone could summon good things her way, it's the Redhead. If anyone had the capacity to call forth good health, it's the Redhead. The mind is a powerful thing. There is merit to having a positive attitude, but no amount of positive-thinking, no amount of summoning good health will ensure one moment of perfect health for any of us.

One day we have breasts that are supple, full of creamy nourishment for our children, breasts which offer comfort and repose for the weary and broken-hearted. Then, we arise one morning to find that those same breasts which brought so much pleasure are the source of a pain so great it threatens our very lives. That such betrayal can happen on a sunny summer's morning when tans are golden, waters so blue, and spirits so light, seems unduly harsh.

Still the Redhead trusts in the one who breathed life into her existence.

"If I had created my own body," she says, "then I would possibly know how to bring about perfect health, but God created it and only God can bring about perfect health."

The Redhead is troubled that anyone would think that if

only they would think rightly, they could be cured of whatever ails them.

"What about the poor souls who aren't healed? That's a heap of guilt to put on them," she says. "To believe that we have that kind of power is a lie from the pit of hell."

Even so there's a temptation to trust in that lie. A sense that if only she can work the equation the right way she can end up with the sum she seeks. That's why when she was first diagnosed the Redhead determined to do all the right things.

"The very first time I was diagnosed I met that moment with every bit of strength, energy, and prayer I could muster. As a family we set out to fight and conquer the cancer."

Initially, the Redhead worried that she had done something, or not done enough of something, to bring this upon herself. She felt guilty. A headstrong woman, she lived life by the rule-book. Rules she made up for herself and for everyone else.

"Two years prior to my diagnosis I was in a place of pretty self-centeredness," she says. "I had high expectations for myself and everyone else. I was definitely not centered on the Lord and what he wanted. I wondered if God needed to bring me to a place where I was focused on him and not on myself."

It's human nature to think we are at fault, at first. The Redhead knows now that her guilt was misguided.

"I'm saddened that I responded that way," she says. Such guilt is a waste of time and energy, essential resources for any person, ill or otherwise. She does not believe that God inflicted her with the cancer as a means of arm-twisting her into submission to his will. That is not the nature of God. Nor did she, as some might argue, attract the cancer to herself.

In 2003, she learned that the cancer had metastasized to the bones. The can-do spirit that had undergirded that first diagnosis dissolved into cries of desperation.

"Ed and I wrapped ourselves in each other's arms and cried ourselves to sleep every night for a month," the Redhead recalls. "Weary with fear, loss, and exhaustion, we could do nothing but trust God for what was to come. The day we fell asleep with dry pillows was a turning point, for we began to once again have hope."

It was a different sort of hope. One that said, whatever befalls, still we trust. That's when the Redhead says she stopped her striving.

"Up until then, I was very focused on fighting the disease. I was doing everything possible to eradicate it. I felt that my hard work and my dependence on the Lord would cure me."

She'd been trying to work the long equation again.

"I've always been about that. Tell me the right answer and I'll do it forever. I just wanted to know the right answer to the dilemma once and for all."

After the cancer spread to her bones, she understood that there would be no right answer.

"I realized no matter how much education I had, no matter how great the doctors were, no matter how well I ate, or how positive my thinking, I lacked the resources to have any influence on my mortality. God alone set every minute of my life."

The Redhead loves her life. She wants to live to see her daughter graduate from high school, from college, and be there when she walks down the aisle. She wants to hold her grandbabies not-yet-born, to teach them how to swim and row a canoe and arrange flowers in a vase.

But the cancer has spread further, to her liver and lungs. She has a cough that won't subside even in the thick air of August.

She can't laugh as deeply as she once did, or take daily prayer walks around the neighborhood any more.

She still cries, of course. It's only natural. God cups his hands to receive those tears. He never tells her to "Buck up, get over it." That's not his nature.

The Redhead continues to pray for healing.

"I pray for complete healing from the cancer that now fills my bones, liver, and lungs."

She pours over God's Word, not in search of some magical incantation she can recite that will shoo away all the evil spirits that threaten her, but to better learn who God is and his hope for her.

People often remark about what a tough warrior she is, how brave and strong.

"It is work, hard work, learning about this disease, my body, making medical decisions," she says. "It is hard work to be disciplined to learn and give my body the optimum nourishment, exercise, and rest it needs. But it has never felt like a fight because God has done the battling."

Instead of summoning riches and good health, the Redhead has learned to summon God's presence. As the cancer continues its invasive march throughout her body, God saturates her soul with the knowledge that she is already healed. That, she says, is why Christ suffered as he did — so that she would know an eternal healing.

A healing so complete that fear has no power over it.

"God loves me so completely that I often wake in the middle of the night singing praises to my King and each morning the same," she says. "I wake with a heart of gratitude for the day and filled with hope for the way God is going to manifest Himself in my life or that of another."

She lives each day expectantly. The way we all should.

She looks for opportunities to testify, not in a preachy way, but in love. When she learns that a doctor's mother is ill, she buys a rose and writes the doctor a card. When she learns that another has just been diagnosed with breast cancer, she stops in the Costco parking lot to pray with this woman she barely knows.

"I delight and expect encounters with others at the produce counter, in parking lots, at the bank and in my workplace for I know that they are not by chance but are instead divinely appointed, designed by God for the benefit of his children, myself included, and for his glory," the Redhead says. "There is nothing more rewarding than to know that God has given me the privilege to be a vessel for his purpose."

Nothing more rewarding.

She clings to the knowledge of that, especially now that her husband Ed has lost his job.

Just when you think it can't get much worse, it can.

The Redhead takes a cocktail of drugs. There's a chemotherapy pill that she takes daily, and a bone booster pill. And a drug that she gets intravenously that fights the growth factor in the cells. It can't differentiate between good cells and bad ones, though, so it just attacks them all.

Sometimes she has to have a blood booster shot, when her blood count gets too low. That shot alone costs a thousand dollars. Sometimes she takes pills that help her sleep comfortably. She has to have x-rays and bone scans and blood draws. All of these things cost money. A lot of money. Thankfully, the bulk of it has been covered by the insurance. That was one worry she didn't have before — how they would pay for such treatment.

But then her husband lost his job. Not because of any

wrongdoing on his behalf. He has been a good and faithful company employee for thirty years. Two more years and he could retire, comfortably, with health benefits. He was looking forward to that.

He worked for a big company. The kind of company whose logo is found on cardboard boxes and the sides of long-haul trucks, nationwide. A seemingly secure company. There was plenty enough to trust God for without this happening.

Six weeks after the Redhead learned the cancer had spread to her liver and lungs, Ed came home and sat down in his favorite leather chair. She was resting in a chaise lounger, reading.

"My job is being terminated," he said. The words were parsed out in a deliberate and calm way. If he felt any sense of panic, he did not show it. Ed was prayed up. He was determined to not add one nanosecond of anxiety to the Redhead's life.

Even when she was at her healthiest, the Redhead did not indulge bad news of any sort. She read only happy books and watched only light-hearted movies. She steered clear of controversy and politics and back-biting.

"I am a baby and I don't like things to be hard or sad and especially not tragic for myself or anyone I love or anyone that I don't even know," the Redhead says. "I am thankful that I know this truth about myself. Being frail and weak to the core has made me deeply dependent upon God's strength. I seek to hear the voice of God, and knowing his character is trustworthy, obedience comes more easily."

Her family responded the same way they had after the dream that startled me awake in 1998 — they gathered together and prayed.

"Our prayer was simple," the Redhead says. "God please lead us on in your grace, fulfill your promise to provide for our every need, and let us reveal your hope, resting in you without anxiety."

The Redhead quotes one of her favorite verses — "Trust in the Lord with all your heart, and lean not on your own understanding. In all your ways acknowledge Him, and He shall direct your paths. Do not be wise in your own eyes; fear the Lord and depart from evil. It will be health to your flesh, and strength to your bones" (Prov. 3:5–6 NKJV).

The Redhead does not seek a mansion made of marble. She does not lust for the luxury of a Lexus. She does not pant after Prada. She does not long for a Rolex to keep track of her remaining hours.

She does not treat God as if he is her personal assistant. She does not order him to go fetch her this thing or that. She does not expect God to be her personal banker. She does not order him to make direct deposits into her account. God is not her genie. He is not her magician. God is not her personal trainer. He is not even her wellness physician. But God is her hope and her assurance. He is her comfort and provider.

★

On June 20, 2009, during the last hours of her life, the Redhead summoned me. She had refused all pain medication, preferring instead to approach death in the same wide-eyed manner that she had her life.

"Don't cry for me," she said. "I am in no pain. God's provision is perfect. His joy complete."

She had learned the real secret that the apostle Paul spoke of, the lesson of being content, of trusting in the God that loved her completely.

No matter what.

THE ENTREPRENEUR

Michael Bienes made millions doing business with Bernie Madoff. Millions. He and business partner, Frank Avellino, were known as "feeders." Bienes, a licensed accountant, and Avellino referred clients to Madoff in exchange for a small cut.

"A business in millions, a profit in pennies," Bienes says, explaining his dealings in a 2009 interview with *Frontline* correspondent Martin Smith. "We were never pigs about it. That's the one thing that kept us going. We were never pigs."[1]

Bienes didn't consider it gluttonous even when he and Avilleno were skimming ten million annually working as unlicensed investment advisors and dealing in unregistered securities — all with Madoff.

It wasn't complicated or even hard work. Bienes said the money he made from his illicit partnering with Madoff was "Easy-peasy. Like a money machine."

He never questioned how it was Madoff could turn out such high returns for his clients. Bienes never asked to see the books. Never verified how it was that Madoff was able to offer a 20 percent return even in a down economy. Bienes idolized Bernie Madoff. With good reason. "He was my income. He was my life." But Bienes did wonder why it was that he was so fortunate, so blessed, so dadgum rich.

"And then I came up with an answer," Bienes said. "My wife and I came up with an answer — God wanted us to have this. God gave us this."

★

Knowing what we do now about that evildoer, Bernie Madoff, such a remark by Bienes seems the height of arrogance and sheer stupidity.

Yet, I'm just as guilty of this sort of wrong-headed thinking as Bienes was, as you probably are. We can't help ourselves. As Americans this sense of entitlement is our inheritance. Entitlement theology may very well be the bastard-child born from the mating of Calvinism's strong work ethic with capitalism's get-all-the-goods-you-can mentality.

According to many, capitalism is the perfect mechanism for carrying out the will of God. It's the equivalent of the confessor's magic lantern. Rub the lantern between two palms, repeat aloud the right incantation, and voilà, the very thing you wish for is spoken into being.

As you may have guessed by now, I don't ascribe to Word of Faith as a rule. Not as a philosophical worldview, at any rate. But when it comes to the daily practice of living the Christian life, buddy, I'm as self-serving as the next bloke doing business on Wall Street.

When I get the $90 blouse on sale for $20, my first thought is, "Thanks, God. I needed that." When one of my essays is picked up by national media, I'm convinced it's because God is "expanding my territory, widening my influence." When my husband's MRI came back clear for a brain tumor, I couldn't help but feel "God's favor" on our lives. And when I was three cars back from the mobile home blown off Interstate 40 by strong winds, and the semi carrying half of that double-wide jackknifed, I knew the reason I escaped unscathed was because of "God's protective hand" over me. I even said a prayer to that effect as I eased on past that truck driver splayed out in the road while he waited for the ambulance crew to arrive.

Our warped way of thinking about God and his favor upon us is insidious and pervasive and downright intrusive. All too often the way we think about God is based upon our good fortune, or lack thereof, and not at all based upon the character of God or upon biblical truths or even upon rational observation. If good things are happening for us, then God must be doing the happy dance. If not, then obviously God is ticked off and it's up to us to figure out why so we can get him to do the happy dance again. That's what leads the Grill Man to conclude that if he doesn't get rich it's because of something he failed to do.

We have a role-reversal issue going on. Instead of recognizing God as our Creator and responding to him as such, we keep fashioning him into whatever role we need him to be playing at the moment. We badger him about toying with our affections when in truth it's us who are being totally capricious about this relationship between creation and Creator. We're the ones who keep trying to fashion God into a puppet that we can control.

Paul Young, author of *The Shack*, says for many it's all about vying for power:

> Many think that a relationship with God is the utilization of the right methods and techniques, bowing to the right set of principles and producing enough performance and obedience to reach the invisible mark of being able to tell God to do what is in our best interests.

Whether it is the legalism of performance or the legalism of having enough faith, it all boils down to one simple reality, we are exchanging relationship for magic. If I have enough "faith" or do enough of the right things (prayer, giving, reading Scripture, attending church, etc.), then God is obligated to perform his part in response. The great Vending Machine God. In relationship you enter a mystery and lose control, two things we are apt to avoid.

Control is at the center of all this constant tension and perpetual striving that makes up the bulk of our lives. It's not really money we are seeking — it's the power. The choices money affords us.

★

It was pouring down rain in Atlanta. I mean pouring. Frogs were drowning, it was raining so hard. It was March, 2009. My car was packed to the hilt with all the necessities that a year of deployment requires — sleeping bag, beach chair, books, laptop, shorts, and a winter coat. What I didn't have, however, was an umbrella. Hey. I'd been living in the Southeast for a year, not in Portland. I reasoned the only umbrella I needed was a beach umbrella and it was packed away in the trunk somewhere.

The year of my deployment, as my husband and I took to calling it, consisted of a couple of different writer's gigs, one near an Army base. But those tours were finished and I was slowly making my way back to Oregon (I'm never in a hurry to leave the South). My sister, Linda, had joined me for the road trip.

Linda and I had this routine. I'd drive while she'd scout the road signs in search of the nearest Starbucks (which also helps explain why the trip was slow). Despite the hard rain, Linda saw the tell-tale sign up ahead and motioned for me to turn. I pulled into the parking lot and parked the car. Linda informed me that she wasn't about to get out of the car without an umbrella. She'd curled her hair, after all.

So I backed the car up and headed for the drive-up, when Linda yelled, "STOP!"

She liked to have scared me half-to-death. "What?" I asked, startled.

"Look at that!" she said, pointing to a white car with a big chrome grille. "It's a brand new Rolls Royce! I've never seen a brand new Rolls 'cept on TV. Oh my gosh, I have to get a picture." Linda proceeded to roll down the window and snap a shot with her cell phone, then my camera.

To be completely honest, I wouldn't know a Rolls from a Towne Car. I'm ignorant that way. When somebody asks me what kind of car drove away from the crime scene, I respond two ways, by size and color. Big or little. Black or red. But Linda, she pays attention to these things.

She also pays attention to God. If my sister is praying for you, you'd better watch out. God listens to her. She is the most praying woman I've ever known. She immediately started praying for the person with the Rolls. What she prayed went something like this: "God, if we've just missed an opportunity to meet someone that you wanted us to meet, please open the door."

I rolled my eyes and muttered some tasteless remark under my breath about the Prayer of Jabez and widening territory again. My sister drives me nuts. She prays over getting a good deal on wallpaper and new shoes on sale. She prays for God's favor, constantly, for her children, her husband, and even, yes, her wayward sister.

I'm not like that. I fear prayer is like a token to be redeemed. I don't want to use it until I'm sure I'm going to get something of real value from it. I save my prayers for the biggies, like an end to war in Iraq and Afghanistan. Or help for the starving children of the Sudan or Rwanda. The truth is, I'm an intellectual elitist about prayer whereas Linda, well, she's like the laundry woman of prayer. She's not afraid to get down and dirty with God. You should see the calluses on her knees. I'd never tell her because she'd get the big head, but I envy her ability to pray about just anything. I wish I could quit filtering my prayers.

While Linda was praying for God's favor, I was placing our order at the drive-up.

"Anything else?" the Starbucks lady asked after I'd ordered the Venti Green Tea Lemonade, sweetened, of course.

"Yeah," I said. "I want to know who owns that Rolls in the parking lot."

It was a Sunday morning in the South. Nothing else was open. So I figured whoever owned it must be in the coffee shop.

"Oh. That's Mark. He's a regular," she replied, casually. "Why, you looking for a sugar daddy?"

"No," I replied, laughing. "I'm happily married. I was just wondering."

"Well, he's got somebody anyway," she said.

"What's he do?" I asked.

"He's a writer."

"Really?" I said. "What does he write?"

"I dunno. Hey Mark, what do you write?"

By this time I was pulling the car forward and telling Linda to get one of my books from underneath the pile of stuff in the backseat. Linda was already up on her knees, moving pillows, chairs, and bags of pork skins.

Passing our drink order over, the Starbucks gal said, "He writes real-estate books."

"Real-estate books?" Turning to Linda I said, "Apparently, I write the wrong kinds of books. He's driving the Rolls and I'm driving the car with the broken driver's-side window." Rain soaked my left side. I placed the drinks in the cup holders and signed over my latest book to Mark, the real-estate guru. A young man waved thanks from inside the dry Starbucks as Linda and I drove off.

I give away a lot of books. I figured I'd never hear from him again. But about four weeks after I returned to Oregon I got an email from Mark's assistant, Amanda. She said her boss wanted to send me a thank-you note for the book I gave him at Starbucks.

I didn't even know people still wrote thank-you notes, especially not to complete strangers. I wrote Amanda back, "Tell your boss I have a deal for him. He agrees to be interviewed for my next book and I'll send him my address so he can thank me properly."

The phone rang this morning as I was wrapping up this book about God and money. I wasn't even surprised. I told you God listens to my baby sister. I'd done some research on Mark, the DM. That's his official title. The DM stands for Deal Maker.

He's young, thirty to be exact, and he has a semi-truckload of money. I knew one more telling detail about Mark and it was the reason I really wanted to interview him. He'd been to Haiti to work with the poor. Why? I wondered. What compelled him?

What I didn't know until we talked was that, like me, Mark had grown up in a trailer park too. The only thing he ever heard his parents argue about was money.

"Because there was never enough of it," Mark says.

He was created with an entrepreneurial spirit and by second grade was running yard sales. He got in trouble in high school when he refused to do the assigned task of filling out a job application. Mark always knew he would never work for others. He intended to be his own boss.

He bought his first business one month out of high school, at age eighteen — a seamless gutter business — for $50,000. The fact that Mark didn't have any money to buy a business or that he didn't know anything about the gutter business, other than "water runs downhill," didn't deter him at all.

"I was more afraid of what I saw daily, seeing people live in the cycle of being broke," he says.

He's never really kept track of it, but if Mark had to guesstimate, he figures he made his first million by the time he was twenty-five, but it's not about the money for Mark.

"I start everything with the end in mind," he says. "It wasn't about chasing the million dollars; it was about chasing the freedom the money gives you."

It's about controlling your own life. Nowadays, Mark has clients who pay him upwards of $100,000 to teach them how to gain that control. When he first started pulling in the big bucks, it created a lot of discord for his family. They were sure that anyone raised up as he had been, making that much money, must be dealing drugs. His grandmother told him how his grandfather had to work three jobs to support his family. She prodded Mark to open up, confess his wrongdoing, and make his life straight.

He laughs about it now, but it's not really all that funny when you think about it. Here he was, working as hard as he knew how, trying to live a life with integrity, following the Golden Rule of doing unto others the way you want them to do unto you, the way his daddy had taught him to do, and his family figured him for a drug dealer.

Mark believes in treating people with respect. It's one of his core values. Those Midwestern values embedded in him as he grew up. Mark is always very aware of how very fortunate and blessed he's been. He thinks being grateful is part of the key to his success. That's why he really likes Joel Osteen. He's a good motivational speaker who Mark says has probably helped a lot of people.

"I think he gives people hope."

We all need that.

But Mark is annoyed with people who curry to a sense of entitlement. People who believe they deserve better or are owed better develop a victim mentality when they don't get what it is they think they ought to be getting. They are rarely grateful and almost always bitter.

When it comes down to it, it's not about how much money you have, but about the kind of person you choose to be. Mark has been through all that rigmarole of figuring out who his real friends are and who feigns friendship simply because they want to be part of his lifestyle. He's done the prodigal son party scene and grown weary of that.

He's had enough money for long enough to figure out that money in and of itself is actually a pretty worthless pursuit. The question that haunts him now is about the kind of legacy he will create for himself and for the family he hopes to have one day.

He's been to Haiti to work with the poor. He's had friends here in the US who've ended up homeless. "Being homeless is not anybody's choice, ever," he says. Mark knows that there are a lot of homeless people who are "way smarter than me." Knowing that makes him even more appreciative of all that he has.

It's a gift — this ability to amass stuff.

It's also a responsibility.

He's trying to figure out what that means for his life, because it isn't enough in life to have all this stuff. Not for Mark it isn't. If he's been given this gift, and he believes he has, then the Giver must have some expectation of him as well, right?

"Now it's about living the legacy," he says. "Creating the full-circle life. I've been at the stage where all I wanted to do was make money, but that's empty now. It's not fun. My main objective now is to be able to give back more."

Mark has friends who live by the 90-percent, 10-percent rule. They live off 10 percent of their earnings and give away 90 percent. Reverse-tithers, he calls them.

Real happiness for Mark comes from "doing the right thing even if it hurts. At the end of the day, that's the type of guy I am."

He's witnessed real miracles in his lifetime that have nothing to do with money. He tells the story of his grandfather, who for eight years never spoke a single word because he suffered from Alzheimer's. The old man sat straight up on his death bed, turned to his wife, and said "I love you" and then drew his last breath.

That's not just a quinky-dink as far as Mark is concerned. "There's something way higher out there."

His business partner is a Believer but Mark has never been one to do something just because others have done it. He has to know it for himself. He believes in a Creator. He just doesn't know yet what his role is in relationship to that Creator. That's what he's trying to figure out.

"I'm going through that learning curve in my life right now."

Mark has moved beyond wrestling with matters of the flesh

and is now wrestling with matters of the spirit. I don't know what the end result will be in Mark's life, but I warned him that my sis was praying for him. And then he mentioned something about how so many people could do so much better financially if they would just trust the power they really have within.

"They want to know everything before they do anything, when they already know enough to make a decision," Mark said. "They just want to know all the 'what ifs.'"

"Listen to yourself, Mark," I said. "That's how it is with faith too. You know enough to make a decision. You just are worried about the what ifs and what that might mean for you."

We are all like Mark in that regard. Many of us aren't willing to wrestle with matters of the Spirit as intently as he is. Many of us are too caught up wrestling with matters of the flesh still. We are more worried about fiscal matters than we are about what really matters.

I heard Pastor Ken Wytsma of Antioch Church in Bend, Oregon, give a sermon titled "Divine Conspiracy" in which he talked about this struggle of ours. Wytsma said that for many, Christianity amounts to an "easy Believism" or "Cultural Christianity." He traces it back to a shift in evangelism that started with Charles Finney in the 1800s, when salvation became more of a matter of numbers and not a condition of the heart.

A kind of Abacus Evangelism. (My terminology, not Wytsma's). One minute we're a red bead on the nonbeliever side, then we utter the prayer of confession and a giant hand moves us down the steel rod to join up with all the other blue Believer beads. The problem with this sort of Christianity is that we never get to be much more than a brightly colored bead and our faith remains pretty wooden.

When confronted with issues of social justice or our obligation to help the poor, or to give up our stuff, we refuse to budge.

"Those of us who bought into Cultural Christianity, it really hits us in the gut," Wytsma says. We don't like people, especially pastors, getting all up in our business that a'way.

You know how many bestselling books there are out there instructing people how to become broke and broken for God? Or how to live as reverse-tithers? Yeah. I checked. Not many. There's no room for such books among the dozens of bestsellers on how to get rich God's way.

Wytsma said issues of social justice ought to be commonplace for Christians. Yet, too often, Wytsma said, our reaction is, "Whoa, whoa, whoa. I'm already a Christian. I'm already forgiven. God already loves me. I'm going to heaven. Don't you ask for my stuff!"

Somewhere along the line we've grown confused. We've started mistaking Christianity for capitalism. If this trend continues, perhaps instead of calling ourselves Christians, maybe we ought to call ourselves Consumptionists.

We've been lollygagging along, convinced that God whistles happily while we head off to work and to play and to shop. We've raised our children among the glitter of M.A.C. and the glitz of Abercrombie. Seniors in high school can't identify which tree is a maple and which one is a birch, but they can tell the difference between a shirt bought from Patagonia and one purchased from Title Nine.

We do all this so mindlessly, convinced that somehow this is God's will for those living in the land of the free (but grossly indebted).

My friend Mandy says this kind of selfish pursuit is an affront: "The idea that God's will must involve following one's dreams contradicts Scripture and disrespects the millions of impoverished Christians around the world who labor every day to provide for their families."

Hard as it is to admit it, not everyone gets a shot at the American Dream, and more than a few have woken to find out that the dream they pursued so relentlessly cost them more than they ever imagined. Throughout Scripture God uses dreams primarily to compel us to seek after him. I can't think of one single instance where he uses a dream to tell somebody to go buy a bigger chariot with four-wheel drive, in case of snow.

The Marine says that the problem with having the poor among us it that they are proof positive that the American way doesn't work for everyone. Those cracks that people fall through? Those aren't cracks, those are dangerous precipices. Fall off just once, and without the help of others, you may never be able to stand on sure-footing again.

We spend a lot of time in this nation talking about pulling ourselves up by our bootstraps. We want to believe that the formula works for everyone: Our obedience + God's favor = unlimited wealth.

But it's a flawed formula.

Some people work hard their entire lives without ever getting ahead. Some people trust God with their whole heart, mind, body, and soul, yet they still can't afford a car or medical insurance. Some, like my dear Redheaded friend, die too young, even though they believe God for healing.

It's not God who's creating the problem. It's us. We're trying to fashion our relationship with God into a sum-ending equation in which we always come out ahead.

We can continue to live out our wooden faith like beads on a rod, and God will be duty-bound to accept us into his gated community because we've prayed the confessor's prayer. But Michael Spenser had it right. The Bible doesn't leave us in the dark about money or about what God expects from us. In fact, it couldn't be any clearer: "Pure and undefiled religion before God and the Father is this: to visit orphans and widows in their trouble, and to keep oneself unspotted from the world" (James 1:27 NKJV).

Sister Schubert is doing just that with Sasha's Home in the Ukraine. So is the Marine and Love Wins Ministry. The Redhead's example continues to encourage us all, as does that of the Ambassador and the Missionary, and yes, despite himself, even the Mayor. There are plenty of others. The Mentoring Project (mentoringproject.org) comes to mind. Founded by author Don Miller, the Mentoring Project addresses our nation's crisis of fatherlessness. Dry Bones in Denver (drybonesdenver.org) ministers to homeless teens. The Hands and Feet Project (handsandfeetproject.org) is building homes in Haiti.

There are unemployed blokes, retired people, urban hipsters, and even, by golly, people in the banking business who are out getting their hands dirty in all kinds of good ways. Remember Larry Wilson? The journalist and film producer who volunteers with Los Angeles Union Rescue Mission? Larry knows a fellow who is a thirty-one-year veteran with Merrill Lynch, who also volunteers at the mission. Asked why he was willing to give up his time and his money in such a manner, the volunteer said it's because of what he learns from people he meets: "They're here because of circumstances that would have caused most of us to fold our tents before we got here. When I see what they overcome, I know there is hope for everyone."

Hope for everyone.

That's the message of Christ.

The message that we ought to be broadcasting to the world through our lives.

If there is a secret to living your best life now, it's this: Stop imagining all the ways in which the universe can serve you and start figuring out how you can serve others. Partner with a ministry in your neighborhood. Become a world-changer. Meditate on the advice from the disciple Matthew: "Seek ye first the kingdom of God, and his righteousness; and all these things shall be added unto you" (Matt. 6:33 KJV).

Consider for a moment that the passage from Matthew has nothing to do with how much wealth you can amass if only you'd master the formula for the Big Life God's way. Quit trying to figure out how to improve the value of your net worth and start figuring out how to make your life truly count for Christ.

The Marine got it right when he told Lena he couldn't pay her light bill for her but he would come over and sit with her when they cut her lights out. That's exactly what God would have us do, and it's exactly what he's promised to do for us. God has offered to sit with us through all of our dark nights, and to stay at our side through the white hot of noonday too. That's how it is with God.

The Song of Zechariah in the Book of Common Prayer puts it this way:

> And, thou, child, shalt be called the prophet of the Highest, for thou shalt go before the face of the Lord to prepare his ways; to give knowledge of salvation unto his people for the remissions of their sins, through the tender mercy of our God, whereby the dayspring from on high hath visited us; To give light to them that sit in darkness and in the shadow of death; and to guide our feet into the way of peace.

Peace, not prosperity, is what we ought to be pursuing.

But if it's a secret you seek, here it is: God's favor is found in his unyielding faithfulness and his eternal devotion to a people unworthy.

Such favor cannot be measured in dollars and cents.

It's priceless.

DISCUSSION QUESTIONS

INTRODUCTION

Have you ever passed by a homeless person? What were you thinking?

What's your definition of community?

What's your responsibility toward community?

CHAPTER 1: THE EVANGELIST

When Jesus said he wanted us to have an abundant life (John 10:10), what did he mean?

Based upon what the Gospels tell us about Jesus, what does it appear his definition of success was?

Who was more successful, John the Baptist, King Herod, or Pontius Pilate? Explain.

CHAPTER 2: THE SISTER

Have you ever eaten a Sister Schubert roll? What did you think?

How do you rate yourself on a scale of 1 – 10 (ten being high) on your awareness of the needs of others?

What's a recent example of your reaching out to meet the needs of others?

When's the last time meeting someone else's need required you to make a sacrifice?

CHAPTER 3: THE CHILDREN

What do you think an anointing is?

Who are some biblical examples of people being anointed? What is it they were anointed to do?

How do you see a child evangelist in light of Paul's instruction regarding pastors and teachers?

Where do we cross the line in exploiting a child in the name of faith?

CHAPTER 4: THE MAYOR

Have you ever asked your pastor why he got into the ministry?

Do you find yourself keeping score regarding other people's vices?

What do you think Jesus wanted us to learn from his instructions to judge not (Matt. 7:1–2)?

Have you ever befriended someone like the Mayor? Would you?

CHAPTER 5: THE AMBASSADOR

What do you keep in your Mason jars?

The Ambassador talks about when he fell away from his faith during his military service. Has there been a time in your life when you fell away from your faith?

What was the cause of that? What brought you back?

In what ways have you manipulated others or taken advantage of them, like the store owner with the brooms?

Outside of church, when was the last time you bore witness to the reality of Christ in your life?

CHAPTER 6: THE LAWYER

What are three things you'd do if someone left you $2.5 million?

What does your view of your finances and your financial goals reveal about your value system?

Have you ever chosen a church to network with for personal or financial gain?

Have you ever had someone at work do you wrong for their own financial gain?

How did you respond to that? Anything you wish you'd done differently?

CHAPTER 7: THE VETERAN

In honor of Butterbean, what are some great dog names you recall?

Do you live your life with a sense of purpose? If so, what is that purpose?

Have you ever wished you were dead, the way the Veteran did? What made you feel that way? What brought you out of that despair?

CHAPTER 8: THE BEAUTICIAN

Who sends money to television evangelists? What do they think they are sending the money for?

Sixty-one percent of those polled said they believe God wants to prosper us. What do you believe?

In what ways are you guilty of trying to manipulate God?

How much do you think God cares about yours or America's financial prosperity?

Can you pray or give your way to wealth?

When is giving really giving to God?

CHAPTER 9: THE MOGUL

*The Mogul liked to cut corners. He wanted to be the biggest, but he wasn't concerned with being the most excellent.
In what ways have you cut corners? What made you think it was worth it?*

Our lives are God's gift to us. If we give less than our best, are we robbing God? Or ourselves?

The Mogul was never satisfied, no matter how much he acquired. In what areas of your life are you never fulfilled? Why is that?

CHAPTER 10: THE BOOKSELLER

Have your finances ever gotten so far out of control that you were in danger of losing your business or your home? What steps did you take to stop the hemorrhaging?

Have you ever been betrayed by a business partner or a friend? How did you handle that?

Are we expected to forgive such deep betrayals? If so, how do we do that?

What should we pray when praying for our enemies?

CHAPTER 11: THE JUBILEE

Consider Leviticus 25: 8 – 17. Contrast the biblical definition of Jubilee to that of the current teachings in the church regarding Jubilee. How do they differ?

Why did God create a year of Jubilee?

How do you think God regards a nation that compromises only 5 percent of the world's population but uses up a third of the world's resources?

What does it mean not to oppress others?

CHAPTER 12: THE MARINE

What are some misconceptions you have about the homeless?

Can everyone pull themselves up by their bootstraps? Is America really a land of equal opportunity?

What is our obligation to the poor? And should our response to the poor only be about obligation? Or should it be about something other than that?

If pure religion is taking care of widows and orphans as mentioned in James 1:27, how undefiled is your religion?

When is the last time you sat with someone in the dark?

Have you ever loved someone the way the Marine talked about? Somebody who couldn't do anything for you?

CHAPTER 13: THE PREACHER

Is having confidence in Christ, that kind of confidence Paul talks about in Philippians 3:12, the same as claiming things in Christ's name?

Is it okay to lay claim to houses or cars or city stadiums in the name of Christ?

The New Testament does say that Christ came to reveal a mystery (Eph. 3). What is the secret Jesus came to reveal?

Michael Spencer says that Joel Osteen is a good motivational speaker, but that he should not say that he is preaching Jesus. Do you agree or disagree? Why or why not?

What makes Joel Osteen's person and message so popular?

Why does the church hold these kinds of preachers in such high esteem?

CHAPTER 14: THE GRILL MAN

What's your preferred style of barbecue?

The Grill Man says that he tithes because God will reward him for it. Is that biblical?

What does the Grill Man mean when he says he's trying to position himself so that when the floodgates open, he's ready?

In what ways do you practice Voodoo Christianity — a beliefism that seeks to manipulate God so that we get what we want?

Were we created and were we saved so that we can get more stuff?

CHAPTER 15: THE GIVER

What would your family think if you chose to spend thirty years living in a 550-square-foot apartment? What would you think of your own child if they did that?

Why do we equate success with the amount of stuff we possess and the square-footage of our homes?

How do you think God views the Giver?

Is there a Giver in your life? How has that person ministered to you?

CHAPTER 16: **THE MISSIONARY**

Is it good evangelical theology to care about the physical well-being of people in other nations? Or does it just make a person a liberal?

What does the following statement mean: "He is no fool to give up that which he cannot keep to gain that which he cannot lose"?

During the time span of the average church service, 700 children will die of hunger, 250 from drinking unsafe water, and 300 will die due to malaria. Should these statistics concern us personally? Are they our problem?

What are you doing to alleviate suffering in the world? What can you do?

CHAPTER 17: **THE EMPLOYEE**

What are your thoughts on AIG?

If the country's financial institutions fail due to their own misconduct and lack of regulatory control, should we bail them out?

Some say we have become a post-Christian nation. Is this reflected in our ethics? Are ethics a matter of religion or not?

Should business managers be held to standards of malpractice when their decisions ruin companies?

Is it God's job to take care of us? Even when we individually or as a nation violate his principles?

CHAPTER 18: THE REDHEAD

Have you ever struggled with the death of a loved one? What good is the God of prosperity in such moments?

What do you think is the difference between the power of positive thinking and the power of praise practiced? Are they the same thing? Explain.

What does it mean to say that God's provision is perfect and that his joy is complete?

CHAPTER 19: THE ENTREPRENEUR

How could Michael Bienes believe God was blessing him for doing corrupt things?

In what ways have you, like Bienes, misconstrued God?

Is it blessing enough that God has promised his presence to us? Why or why not?

So much of how we define ourselves is wrapped up in what we own. If you lost it all tomorrow, would you be the same person you are today? Would it make it more difficult to trust Jesus or easier to trust him?

Have the stories in this book challenged your perspective about money and about God? How so?

AUTHOR'S NOTE

THERE ARE SEVERAL MINISTRIES MENTIONED IN THIS BOOK, but one that has captured my heart is a ministry in Raleigh, North Carolina, under the direction of Hugh Hollowell. Here's how Hugh sums it up: Love Wins Ministries shares unconditional love and friendship with the homeless and poor population of Raleigh, North Carolina. We focus on relationships, not outcomes — just like you do with your friendships. If one of our friends wants change in their life, we will help with that however we can. And if they desire no change at all, we will honor that as well. No matter what, they will be loved, respected, and treated as an equal. Because they are.

I wrote about Hugh in the chapter titled "The Marine." A portion of all proceeds from this book will be directed to Love Wins Ministries. You can find out more information about Love Wins at http://lovewins.info.

Sasha's Home in Gorlovka, Ukraine, is dedicated to creating a warm and loving environment for abandoned Ukrainian children. The house serves as a temporary home for the children while they await adoption by their "forever families" and is a better alternative to the overcrowded state institutions. To learn more about how you can help or to contribute to the mission, please visit www.barnesfamilyfoundation.org.

Additionally, if this book has spoken to you about the need to put your own house in financial order, there are several reputable ministries out there that can help. The one mentioned in this book, Crown Financial Ministries, defines their mission this way: "Equipping people worldwide to learn, apply, and teach God's financial principles so they may know Christ more intimately, be free to serve him, and help fund the Great Commission." To learn more about Crown, check out their website at www.crown.org. The Bookseller says participating in Crown was the best investment she ever made.

ACKNOWLEDGMENTS

I WAS TRAVELING THROUGH WILLACOOCHEE, GEORGIA, ONE summer afternoon when the idea for this book first came to me. I'd been to Fort Bragg and Fort Stewart to interview widows from the war in Afghanistan and Iraq. Grief-weary, I said, "One of these days I'm going to write a book called *Will Jesus Buy Me a Double-Wide?*" It was a "Laughter through tears is my favorite emotion" moment.

That this book exists at all is because one person took my pitiful attempt at humor seriously. That person was Andy Meisenheimer, my editor. What Andy would never tell you (but I will) is that he and his wife, Mandy, have the kind of undefiled faith that James refers to. Cultural Christianity would never suit them. They are the kind of people who cry out, "Bring it on, God!"

What I see in Andy and Mandy is that same kind of heart that compelled my in-laws Gene and Gwen to leave the comforts of their Oregon home and travel to the jungles of Ecuador with their young family all those many years ago.

Zondervan is full of people committed to furthering a message that matters and it's an honor to be numbered among their authors. Thank you to Becky Philpott for spit-shining my musings, to Tom Dean, who claims to be a Methodist but does his job with a Pentecostal's fervor, to Jessica Secord, who intimately knows doubles of a different sort, for her unflagging efforts to help spread the word, and to the design team, Laura Mason and Beth Shagene, for bringing their creative juices to this project. My appreciation also goes out to the sales team, full of passionate individuals who work tirelessly to sell these books. A special thank-you to the rally team, Stan Gundry, Dudley Delffs, and Angela Scheff. A shout-out to Jackie Aldridge for her gracious notes and attention to details. Thank you, Joyce Ondersma, for all the hospitality and for letting me steal your NASCAR pin. Thanks also to Melissa for sharing your NAS-CAR tattoo with me. I'm awestruck by you.

Kathie Bennett embraced the message of this book and then boldly took me by the hand and started introducing me to everybody she ran across, including her beautiful, bright, and engaging mama, a woman who has lived her entire life with intention. Thank you, Kathie, for believing in me and in this book, and for pursuing opportunities with relentless and enthusiastic dedication.

This book is full of stories from real people who've lived extraordinary lives. I met some of these people while working as an editorial writer for the *FayObserver* in Fayetteville, North Carolina. I owe a big thank you to editorial page editor Tim White and senior editorial writer Gene Smith, and to the paper's publisher, Charles Broadwell, for their unyielding support of my writing endeavors. There aren't many independently owned newspapers left in the country but the *FayObserver* is one of the best. Thank you, Charles, Tim, and Gene.

For those who so willingly entrusted your faith journey with me, thank you for allowing me the honor of sharing your story with others.

In all the years I've been writing there has never been a more tumultuous time in the publishing business. Many independent booksellers have gone belly up. These booksellers are our neighbors, our friends. They need our support. Buy local.

Thank you to the many people who provided me a comfortable bed, warm shower, and nourishment during the research for this book: Pat & Patti C. Henry, John B. & Stacey Howell, Hazel Howell, Ken & Sherri & Caitlyn Callaway, Jerry & Patti Burke, Frank & Jane Feagin, Jason & Weezie Phillips, Ray & Bev Martin, Gordon & Pam Wofford, and Pablo & Maria Gallegos.

There is a group of friends who pray for me and encourage me: Peggy Wright, JennyLynn Buntin, Lynn Wilkes, Karen Clark, Lillian Champion, Miz Betty Joe Wolfe, Gary Nelson, Brent & Lisa Baldwin, Pam Wofford, Debbie Johnson and all my Wall buddies, especially to Charlie and Red who took special care of me when the Veteran passed.

When the Redhead and the Veteran died, I lost two of my dearest friends and my most fervent prayer warriors. Oh, how I miss them.

In the loneliest of moments, I have a group of author friends whose advice, laughter, and prayers I seek. Thank you Patti Callahan Henry, Michael Morris, Janis Owens, Shellie Tomlinson, Bob Welch, Scot McKnight, Susan Isaacs, and Sandra Conroy.

A shout out to Jordan Green, Chad Gibbs, Penny Carothers, and all my other cohorts in the struggle at the Burnside Writers Collective (burnsidewriters.com). Very gracious of you to allow an AARP member among your hip, cool crowd.

Thank you, Sister Tater, for your prayers, your laughter, and for guiding me to the Starbucks in Atlanta and the King's Ransom in Sedona. You have always been privy to the best parts of my story.

It was Mama who first taught me that Jesus loves me. Thank you, Mama.

It's difficult to measure the merit of life as a writer. There are long days of isolation where it certainly seems like I'm not doing enough to impact the world for Christ, but my guy Tim believes that what I do matters. I hope he's right.

Our amazing offspring, Stephan, Ashley, Shelby, and Konnie and our sons-in-law, Zack and Jon, belong to a generation of Christians who've rejected the plastic Jesus. They want the real thing.

Now if only one of them would give us a grandbaby, we could move into that double-wide in Point Clear, Alabama.

NOTES

INTRODUCTION

1. Destiny's Child, "Survivor" *Survivor*, Sony, 2001.

CHAPTER 1: **THE EVANGELIST**

1. David Van Biema, Jeff Chu, "Does God Want You to Be Rich?" *TIME*, September 10, 2006.

2. "Senate Committee Investigating Six Major Ministries by Ted Olson," *Christianity Today*, November 6, 2007.

3. Eric Gorski, "Do Piety and Profit Mix?" *The News & Observer*, Associated Press, January 22, 2008.

4. "African-American Churches Weigh Gospel Debate," *National Public Radio*, July 31, 2005.

5. Brody Mullins, "RNC Picks up $1 Million after Palin Speech," *Wall Street Journal*, September 4, 2008.

6. Dr. C. Thomas Anderson, *Becoming a Millionaire God's Way* (Mesa, Ariz.: Winword Publishing, Inc., 2004), 69.

7. Ibid., 122.

8. Ibid., 148.

9. Ibid., 149.

10. David Sedaris, *Dress Your Family in Corduroy and Denim* (New York: Little, Brown and Company, 2004), 10–12.

CHAPTER 3: **THE CHILDREN**

1. "Marjoe," Documentary, produced by Howard Smith & Sarah Kernochan (Cinema 10, 1972).

2. Ibid.

3. Ibid.

4. Ibid.

5. Cynthia McFadden and Melia Paria, "Kid Preacher Can't Make a Believer Out of Everyone," ABC News: *Nightline*, May 18, 2009.

6. Ibid.

7. Ibid.

8. Ibid.

9. Ibid.

10. Ibid.

11. David Van Biema and Jeff Chu, "Does God Want You to be Rich?" *TIME*, September 18, 2006.

12. Ibid.

13. Philip Yancey, "It's Hard to Be Like Jesus: Why Would Anyone Choose to Follow a God Who Promises More Hardship, Not Less?" *Christianity Today*, May/June 2005.

CHAPTER 8: **THE BEAUTICIAN**

1. Ames Alexander, "CEO of Ministry Builds $4 Million Lakefront Home," CharlotteObserver.com, June 28, 2009.

2. Ray Chandler, "Chief of Troubled Television Ministry Building $2 Million House in Oconee County," *Independent Mail, South Carolina*, Monday, June 29, 2009. IndependentMail.com.

3. "I-Team Investigates the Inspiration Network," *Local news for Charlotte*, December 2, 2008. WCNC.com.

4. Ibid., 4.

CHAPTER 9: **THE MOGUL**

1. Tony Adams, "Then His Era Ended," *Columbus Ledger-Enquirer*, Sunday, September 28, 2008.

2. Ibid.

3. Alan Judd, "Dealerships Took Risky Road," *Atlanta-Journal Constitution*, Sunday, September 28, 2008.

4. Robert Siegel, "At Auto Show, GM Seeks to Shift Perceptions." www.npr.org/templates/story/story.php?storyId=99253055.

CHAPTER 10: THE BOOKSELLER

1. Mike Odom, "Former Bookstore Employee Out on Bail," *Baldwin County Now*, January 9, 2009, www.baldwincountynow.com.

CHAPTER 12: THE MARINE

1. Thomas Merton, *Seeds of Contemplation* (New York: New Directions, 1949), 107.

CHAPTER 13: THE PREACHER

1. Anderson, *Becoming a Millionaire God's Way*, 132.

2. Victoria Moran, "Joel Osteen at Yankee Stadium: Part 2," *BeliefNet.com*, Monday, April 27, 2009. http://blog.beliefnet.com/yourcharmedlife/2009/04/joel-osteen-at-yankee-stadium-part-2.html.

CHAPTER 17: THE EMPLOYEE

1. Michael de la Merced and Gretchen Morgenson, "A.I.G. Allowed to Borrow Money from Subsidiaries," *New York Times*, September 14, 2008.

2. Amanda Ruggeri, "AIG Gets Fourth Government Bailout after Record Loss," *U.S. News and World Report*, March 2, 2009.

3. Nanette Byrnes, "Damning Capitol Hill Hearings on AIG," *Business Week*, October 7, 2008.

CHAPTER 19: THE ENTREPRENEUR

1. Martin Smith, correspondant, "The Madoff Affair," *Frontline*, May 12, 2009.

Where's Your Jesus Now?

Examining How Fear
Erodes Our Faith

Karen Spears Zacharias

"Where's our confidence? Our hope?
Is it possible that, in our hyper-vigilance
against our enemies, real or perceived,
we've taken our eyes off of Jesus, our
protector and Redeemer?"

Author Karen Spears Zacharias observes that, more and more often, Christians are letting fear blind them to the love of the very God they worship.

Zacharias examines the world around us and the events that shape our lives, weaving a compelling exploration of faith versus fear. How is it that those of us who claim to be so firmly founded can be so easily shaken? How do we believe that a God who loves us more than we can comprehend can be willed by us to harm those who do not share our beliefs?

Writing with passion while avoiding the extremes of contemporary discussion, Zacharias melds social commentary, insightful spirituality, and a rapier wit in a profound meditation on the nature of faith, "the evidence of things not yet seen."

Hardcover, Printed: 978-0-310-28386-7

Pick up a copy at your favorite bookstore or online!

After the Flag Has Been Folded

A Daughter Remembers the Father She Lost to War — and the Mother Who Held Her Family Together

Karen Spears Zacharias

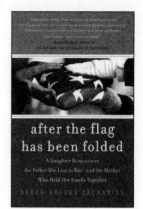

A Woman's Story of Love and Loss

- A timely tribute to those who dedicate their lives to defend their country
- An inspiring story of triumph and redemption

Here is the story of a family left fatherless by a war that shamed a nation and left thousands of children abandoned. This is the uplifting tale of a poor Southern family trying desperately to regroup in the midst of absolute chaos. You will be amazed by one terrified young widow's strength to raise three very confused children, her entire family caught up in a distant war that made absolutely no sense to them.

After the Flag Has Been Folded is an amazing story:

- For every woman, daughter, or son — American or Vietnamese — who lost a husband or father to that war.
- Of reconciliation between a daughter and her father, a daughter and her nation, and a daughter and the people of Vietnam.
- For a country once again touched by the uncertainty of war.

Softcover: 978-0-06-072149-7   Note: Published in hardcover as *Hero Mama*

Pick up a copy today at your favorite bookstore!

HARPER ● PERENNIAL

Share Your Thoughts

With the Author: Your comments will be forwarded to the author when you send them to *zauthor@zondervan.com*.

With Zondervan: Submit your review of this book by writing to *zreview@zondervan.com*.

Free Online Resources at
www.zondervan.com

Zondervan AuthorTracker: Be notified whenever your favorite authors publish new books, go on tour, or post an update about what's happening in their lives at www.zondervan.com/authortracker.

Daily Bible Verses and Devotions: Enrich your life with daily Bible verses or devotions that help you start every morning focused on God. Visit www.zondervan.com/newsletters.

Free Email Publications: Sign up for newsletters on Christian living, academic resources, church ministry, fiction, children's resources, and more. Visit www.zondervan.com/newsletters.

Zondervan Bible Search: Find and compare Bible passages in a variety of translations at www.zondervanbiblesearch.com.

Other Benefits: Register yourself to receive online benefits like coupons and special offers, or to participate in research.